MINI AUSTRALIAN SHEPHERD

Expert Dog Training

MINI AUSTRALIAN SHEPHERD

Expert Dog Training

"Think Like a Dog"

Here's Exactly How to Train Your

Mini Australian Shepherd

PAUL ALLEN PEARCE

ISBN: 9781093185744

What Customers Say About Their Results!

~ - ~ - ~ - 5 Star Reviews - ~ - ~ - ~

5.0 out of 5 Stars! | Awesome Book

"This amazing book told me everything I needed to know to prepare and train my new puppy."

-Chris

5.0 out of 5 Stars! | This is a Fantastic Book!

"I purchased this book to help train my puppy. Very happy that I did! Easy read and entertaining as well. You will not be disappointed!"

- Robin Culver

5.0 out of 5 Stars! | Puppy Training With a Sense of humor!

"Not only was this an easy read, it was humorous. I realized that's the part I'm missing when training a pup - a sense of humor. All steps were clearly outlined in addition to what to do if the first attempts don't work out. This book was a great read and very helpful."

- Pamela Cozart

~ - ~ - ~ - 5 Star Reviews - ~ - ~ - ~

5.0 out of 5 Stars! | How Brilliant This Is

"This is a no nonsense, straightforward instructional training guide for you dog. Anyone who has ever had a puppy knows how brilliant dogs are. You need to understand how they think and react to kindness and challenges. An excellent guide for any dog owner."

- R. A. MOON

~ - ~ - ~ - 5 Star Reviews - ~ - ~ - ~

5.0 out of 5 Stars! | Great Info

"I have had three dogs, and this book was a great reference to go to when I needed help."

-Dotzee

~ - ~ - ~ - 5 Star Reviews - ~ - ~ - ~

5.0 out of 5 Stars! | Five Stars!

"Love this book except I wish I read it before we got the puppy. It has all the information that you will never need and it makes so much sense. The most useful section (in my opinion) is the house training section.

It has tips that the vet told us afterwards and if we read the book before getting the puppy, it would have been so helpful. I made the mistake thinking that I will read it after we got the puppy not realizing that you get no sleep at all the first few weeks and when you are awake, you have no energy at all. This book would have made my life so much easier."

-MJA

Acknowledgments

For my family and friends that have relentlessly supported my many
endeavors.

Table of Contents

Introduction

"We can judge the heart of a man by his treatment of animals." - Immanuel Kant

From the learning curve of training my first dog and the many that followed, this book contains the methods that have successfully worked worldwide for millions of dog owners and trainers including myself.

I know that you will find all of the information inside this training guide easy to follow and informative. My hope is that you have yet to purchase your Mini Australian Shepherd puppy and are buying this guide now to proactively prepare for the introduction of your new furry creature's entrance into your life. Don't worry though, if you already have a grown dog or new puppy at home, it is just as effective.

Though this guide approaches training as a serious endeavor, your dog will teach you otherwise. No doubt, the reason that you are bringing a dog into the family is for the enjoyment of their company, so while focusing on training always feel free to laugh, smile and enjoy the process.

In an attempt to keep you and the book lighthearted, I have added some humor and fun throughout by infusing tales of my dog's playful spirit. I find dogs entertaining, comforting and, at times, like a therapist - thank the universe they are such good listeners.

Reading this instructional guide prior to picking up your puppy will prepare you for its arrival, benefit your new puppy and help you to establish the precise mindset for owning and training a Miniature Australian Shepherd.

Included inside this book's first section is help for new puppy parents that instructs them on how to prepare the house for the new arrival, socialization, treats, clicker training, and how and when to reward their puppy. Additional information also instructs them on how to avoid potential negative behavioral issues by doing the right things, starting on the first day. Prevention is a savior.

The second section educates dog owners in effective Mini Australian Shepherd training techniques. Moreover, how to understand and use canine communication, handle, housetrain, crate train and teach basic commands. Additionally, it contains a puppy's training milestones and guidance for shaping behaviors and problem solving.

Each command is written out in an easy-to-follow, step-by-step format that uses the highly effective reward-based clicker training. However, if you choose not to use a clicker, you can still follow the instructions and train your puppy by using rewards only.

Section 2 also contains instructions on how to solve jumping, barking, nipping and digging behaviors.

The final section delves into basic care and grooming for Mini Aussies, nutrition and some final thoughts about training.

I'm certain that inside you will find complete and concise proven training support featuring highly useful information pulled from years of personal training experience, other professional trainers, various training manuals, research, and years of living with my own canine friends.

Each chapter contained inside this dog-training guide complements the others, and will help to shape your puppy into a well-behaved dog that will be welcomed anywhere and will be a pleasure to be around.

By purchasing this training guide, you will be on your way to securing the necessary tools and knowledge to assure your success as a Mini Aussie dog owner and trainer.

I am confident that you will find this guide effective, easy to understand and fun, so move onto chapter one, "The First Few Days", and get started preparing for the joy-filled journey of dog ownership.

1 The Mini Australian Shepherd

Mini Aussie, Miniature Australian Shepherd, Mini American

I get excited every time I have a chance to train a Mini Australian Shepherd because I know it is going to be a fulfilling experience. I really enjoy training this intelligent and quick-learning breed because they bring such enthusiasm to everything they do. I know you will experience the same.

Charged with liveliness, they are as loyal, endearing a hound as one could come across, and it is always a pleasurable experience to meet one. Their innate exuberance to perform is every dog owner's dream. They are feisty, confident and amicable companions too - what other qualities could a dog family desire from their family's herding pet? The only grievous error an owner can make is to ignore or isolate this breed, thus keeping their many fine qualities from blossoming.

For those unfamiliar with the history of the Mini Australian Shepherd, the common historical account states that the Miniature Australian Shepherd was first developed in California during the mid-1960s from dogs that were smaller than the average Australian Shepherds, but similar in all physical and most personality characteristics. The goal was to continue breeding them for their size, intelligence and their dynamic personalities. Smaller statured Australian Shepherds indeed existed prior to the 1960s, which is why they were available to form mini Australian Shepherds that then became Miniature Australian Shepherds. Mini American Shepherds essentially are Mini Australian Shepherds, but sometimes this is debated in the canine world. The AKC made the decision to rename the Miniature Australian Shepherd, Miniature American Shepherd.

Mini Aussies share almost all of the personality characteristics, coat and eye colors as well as a penchant for herding that their bigger brothers have. In fact, these little dogs are perfect for herding small livestock such as sheep and goats but, if necessary, can also handle larger stock.

If that's not your need, just throw them in the vehicle with you and enjoy their company wherever you wander too.

Intelligent and biddable, they quickly became favored as household pets as well as by those who require their herding proficiencies. They have become quite popular with those that travel with and own horses.

Their size allows them to fit into either urban or rural settings; however, owners must keep them active and exercised. A busy Mini Aussie is a happy Mini Aussie, so try to include them in your daily duties and give them jobs of their own to perform. They are just as wily as full-sized Aussies, so don't be surprised by their problem-solving skills.

Mini Aussies come in a variety of colors such as blue and red merle with or without white or copper trim, black bi or tri that has a solid black body with copper, white or copper and white, red bi or tri with a variance in reds as a base and then copper, white, or both copper and white.

The American Kennel Club (AKC) officially recognized the Miniature Australian Shepherd in 2015, adopting them into the herding category as Miniature American Shepherds. As of 2017, they are ranked the 36th most popular dog registered with the AKC. The AKC standard states their basic colors as 'varying'.

Mini Aussies are quick learners and it is usually easy to train them not only basic commands, but also tricks and sports skills, such as agility, disc dog, herding and Flyball. They are prone to herding and will often attempt to herd small children and other animals so be prepared to do some focused work on acceptable spacing and bumping. They require multiple daily walks or a jog combined with exercises that are more energetic.

Mini Aussies are small-sized dogs that are small enough for apartments and able to cope with smaller living quarters, but only if they are sufficiently exercised. They are usually good with children and other pets, and are versatile, excellent companions, a bit timid towards strangers but not shy and enthusiastic about their tasks. Additionally, they are devoted and protective of their families and outstanding working dogs that have strong guarding instincts with flocks. Their demeanor allows them to adjust to the tasks they are performing by applying the amount of energy and enthusiasm necessary to accomplish the task without losing control.

Due to their natural wariness towards strangers and their exuberance, early and proper socialization is a key component for rearing a healthy-minded Mini Australian. Two of my clients, Brian and Monica, tell the story about their first Mini Australian named Tigre, confirming how too little socialization affected him. Together we were able to turn him into an upstanding canine citizen.

"As busy novice puppy owners we were only able to spend time with Tigre when at home after working, and due to this he was unaware of the many people and places he would later encounter. Unfortunately, this increased his wariness towards strangers and he adopted a heightened sense of territorialism. By the time we realized how severe the problem was, he was about 11 months old and it was difficult to have visitors without some disturbance from him.

After some diagnostic help from Paul, we gradually eased him into open-mindedness, but not until many hours had been spent introducing him to various types of stranger and worldly situation so that he was capable of meeting and greeting people with a calm happy demeanor, and now we can take him anywhere. Now we understand why early and ongoing socialization is a key component to having a healthy dog."

Their grooming needs are minimal. Depending on what your Mini Aussie has been into, a brushing of their medium length coat once or twice a week and an occasional bath is all that is necessary. If your Mini Australian Shepherd is in the field a lot then regularly brushing and combing him to rid him of burrs and to check for critters will help to keep tangles and mats from forming.

Mini Aussies love learning and performing new tricks. If treated well and properly exercised, this is a terrific breed to enjoy, and your dog will stay close by and enjoy your company.

It isn't hard to understand why they are quickly rising in popularity and being warmly welcomed into many homes, but before adding one to your family, please know without a doubt that you are able to meet their daily requirements.

Mini Australian Shepherd Rescue

Miniature Australian Shepherds are often acquired without any clear understanding of what goes into owning one, and these dogs regularly end up in the care of rescue groups, and are badly in need of adoption or fostering. Take the time to understand the breed to ascertain that it is the right fit for your family.

Before adopting a Mini Australian Shepherd, please be certain that you have the time and means to care for a dog. If you have the facilities and ability, please rescue a dog and enjoy the rewarding experience that it offers both of you.

If you are interested in adopting a Mini Australian, a rescue group is a good place to start. I have listed a few below

http://mascusa.org/breed/rescue.html

http://mascaonline.com/finding-an-aussie/rescue-resources/

Quick Facts

Size – Mini Aussies average 13-18 inches in height and 20-40 pounds classifies them in into the small dog category.

Tail – Mini Aussies have a naturally short or docked tail.

Coat – Medium length double coat that requires brushing a couple of times per week and sheds daily.

Personality – They are loyal, intelligent, protective, versatile for work, adaptable to all living conditions, enjoy close family ties and are commonly easy to train.

Competition – Enjoys competing in agility, herding, Flyball and other competitions.

Herding – Great for herding goats, sheep and even larger stock, many horse people solicit the services of this durable little dog.

Health Concerns – Hip dysplasia, hereditary eye defects such as progressive retinal atrophy, and degenerative myelopathy that is a spinal cord disease.

Exercise needs – Daily rigorous exercise is required encompassing more than one outing per day.

2 The First Few Days

"A dog teaches a boy fidelity, perseverance, and to turn around three times before lying down." - Robert Benchley

Bringing Home the Puppy

The time has come to bring your puppy home. There are a couple of things to keep in mind on this day. First, that you are a stranger. Second, that he or she has probably never been in a car or away from its mom or littermates. As you can imagine this will be a stressful moment for your puppy, so try to make the ride home as free of stress as possible.

Before departing the puppy procurement place, allow your puppy to relieve itself, and during the ride provide a soft, comfortable place in a crate or nestled in a person's arms. He may cry or bark during the ride, but that is normal behavior and you must handle it calmly. This will begin to establish that you are there to help. By speaking calmly and evenly, and not speaking harshly, you will show your puppy that you care and are not to be feared.

If possible, bring along the entire family and begin the bonding process during the car ride home. Many times the person that brings the puppy home is the person with whom the puppy will begin to form the tightest bond. Drive straight home so that the pup spends the least amount of time inside the car. Avoid family members over-handling the pup during the ride home; simply comfort the pup.

If you have to stop for a pee/poop stop, be sure to carry your puppy to an area unused by other dogs' eliminations and properly clean up afterward. Your puppy will not have been vaccinated yet and could have worms or parasites in his or her feces and needs to avoid exposure to other dogs' feces that could also contain worms or parasites.

Ride Home Checklist

- Cleaning supplies, just in case.
- Soft towel or blanket.
- Collar – if you use a collar, be sure it is tight. If you can fit one finger between the collar and your puppy's neck, then it has been correctly

tightened. It is good idea to begin the collar adjustment process as early as possible.

- Newspapers, paper towels, and plastic bags.
- A smile, good mood, and cheerful tone of voice.
- Crate (optional).
- Pet odor neutralizer (optional).

After your new puppy has performed his first elimination in the predestinated spot in the yard, then bring him inside, unclip the leash and let him do as he pleases and encounter creatures on his own terms.

Never force yourself or other animals on a pup, allow him to find his own comfort level and make his own decisions about whether to engage. This is the beginning of the all-important socialization process, i.e. place them in the proximity of other creatures and in other circumstances so they have a chance to engage on their own.

If you have other pets around, you should first consider placing your puppy inside a pre-prepared pen so that there is a barrier between him and the others. The first day is all about acclimatizing to new surroundings and people. In addition, you can expect that he will be missing his littermates and mother. Do not over handle your puppy during the first couple of days, allow him time to adjust and engage with others by using his own will.

Beginning with the first day, establish the schedule for feeding and outdoor relief breaks. Every forty-five minutes to an hour take him to his waste elimination spot and see if he needs to pee or poop and, if after a few minutes he doesn't, return inside and try again in about 10-15 minutes.

Don't turn elimination outings into play sessions because you want to train your pup to know that elimination breaks are only for elimination, which avoids being tricked into going outside for fun time. Of course, you can play a bit or let him smell the yard after he eliminates and you can praise him with a "Good boy".

Next, add walks, exercise and training to the schedule, then from this day forward follow that schedule as best you can. Dogs love structure.

Your new puppy will be missing his littermates and mother, so don't be surprised if you hear some whining and whimpering. Your job is to provide support and comfort but do not over-coddle him by running to his side at every little whimper. This separation anxiety will most likely be more prevalent during the nighttime, so keep your puppy close by where you sleep, either next to your bed or at your open doorway.

Relentless pining can be a sign of more serious separation anxiety (SA) and you should quickly attend to him to lessen the symptoms and solve the problem.

Day by day, your pup will adjust to his new surroundings and start to understand that he is loved and cared for by his new family, and then the separation anxiety will begin to decrease. When a pup understands that all of his needs are being met, a human-puppy bond will form and you will automatically become the alpha leader, which will enable him to feel secure and calm.

As you begin teaching your puppy his name, first establish eye contact before saying his name. Remember his name is only to get his attention, not for him to come to you. When issuing commands, say your puppy's name followed by the command, e.g. "Zeke come".

Begin crate training so that he has a safe place to relax and for you to place him when necessary. RULE ONE – your puppy should love his crate so never use it as punishment. If forced to give a time-out, choose a dull place such as a pantry or bathroom. The crate also aids in house-training because dogs are naturally clean and will do everything not to soil their own den/crate.

The first few days you will be busy making regular trips outside for elimination breaks, acclimatizing him to his new surroundings, introducing other creatures, teaching name recognition, beginning crate training, adoring him and keeping him nearby so that you can avoid indoor accidents of all types. Don't forget to supply ample, appropriately sized chew toys.

First Couple of Days and Nights Checklist

- Upon arriving home, take your new pup straight to the predestinated outdoor elimination spot. You will use this spot every time, making it the pup's poop/pee palace.
- Clear the indoor area of other pets and place your puppy down to explore. Do not crowd the puppy and, if children are present, have them provide the puppy with plenty of space. Allow him to come to them under his own initiative. Have everyone remain calm and gentle when interacting with him.
  All puppies act differently. Some take off exploring the house, while others just curl up and survey their surroundings, and some might doze off.
  Another good option is to place your puppy directly inside his gated area that is already prepared with the proper pee pads, a crate with a

blanket inside, a water bottle or small bowl, a blanket outside the crate and a couple of chew toys.

- Keep in mind that if your puppy was flown in or is from a shelter that they may be stressed and be extremely tired from the previous day/night. Expect that the following day they will be rested and livelier.
- Separation anxiety is natural and you might hear your puppy whine, squeal, or howl. They might have difficulty sleeping the first few days or weeks. Your puppy has to get used to being away from his sisters, brothers, and mom, who used to snuggle with him.
- Move slowly when introducing your other pets to your new puppy. A crate, baby gate, or exercise pen puts a barrier between them and allows both to adjust to one another without direct physical contact. I definitely recommend this.
- After about three or four days, take your puppy to the veterinarian for a complete check-up.
- It is very important to show your puppy that they are wanted and cared for. This is of the utmost importance during the first few days.

Elimination Time

- Take him or her out for elimination every half hour. Elimination accidents are common during the first couple of days so clean them thoroughly and use pet deodorizers so that there is no trace. Gradually, after a few days or weeks, pups will be able to increase the length between elimination times.
- Always take them to the designated outdoor elimination spot.
- Do not become angry about elimination accidents. If you see your pup going indoors, if possible, pick him up and let him finish outdoors in the designated spot, and afterward praise him while he's still outdoors.
- Escort your puppy outside and begin praising him when he begins his elimination business, but then let him finish in peace.
- To prevent frequent accidents take notice if you need to shorten the time between elimination trips.
- Track your puppy's schedule regarding eating and elimination as this can help you eradicate accidents and begin housebreaking. Tracking will help you to learn your puppy's patterns.
- After feeding, always take your puppy outdoors.
- Pick up the water bowl around 8pm each night.

- Always praise your puppy when he or she eliminates waste outdoors and not indoors. This will strengthen your bond and begin building trust.
- Before bedtime, always take your puppy out for elimination. A walk will help them to fall asleep.
- Take your puppy out first thing in the morning.
- Allow him to eliminate fully. Most puppies will need to produce several small amounts to complete a full elimination.

"Where does my puppy sleep?"

- The first night will most likely be the most difficult for your puppy, but do not isolate him because he is vocalizing his loneliness. Try not to keep him far from where you are sleeping. He is alone in a strange place, and you want him to feel comfortable and welcomed. For example, do not put him in the garage, basement or far end of the house away from people.
- Options for not isolating your puppy are placing a dog bed or blanket on the floor near your bed, or in his crate near your bed or just outside the open bedroom door. For a variety of reasons, it is advised not to have your puppy in your bed.

Even though your puppy is whimpering, do not pay him too much attention every time he is vocalizing distress. This can become a negative behavior used by the pup to get you to come to him at every request - a habit you don't want to form.

3 Socializing Your Mini Aussie

"If you want the best seat in the house, move the dog." Unknown

Where, When and Why

Everyone reads or hears socialization mentioned when researching about dogs. What is the reason for socialization? When is the best time to socialize a shiny new puppy? Is it just about them getting along well with other dogs and people, or is there more to it? Do I let my puppy loose with other puppies, just sit back, and watch? These and many more questions are often asked, so let me provide the answers.

Socialization is for your dog to learn and maintain acceptable behaviors in any situation, especially when the adult dog or puppy does not want to engage. The goal is for your puppy to learn how to behave in any normal situation that occurs in life without becoming overly stimulated, fearful, reactive or aggressive. No matter what the circumstance, your dog should be able to go with the flow, keep centered and remain calm. The proper socialization of your puppy is a crucial part of their training and a life-long process.

Exposure to the many things we think are normal are not normal to our little puppies or adult dogs. Mechanical noises, such as lawnmowers, car horns, blenders, coffee machines, dishwashers, stereos, televisions, garbage trucks, and other similar items make noises that dogs have to adjust too.

As well as mechanical noises, they will also be exposed to other living creatures represented by other household pets, strange dogs, cats and critters in the yard, such as gophers, rabbits, squirrels, and birds. Further, dogs must become accustomed to family members, friends, neighbors and, of course, the dreaded strangers.

All of the things mentioned above and more are new to most six or eight-week-old puppies, so immediately begin their gradual introduction to these items and living creatures.

Continually remain alert to your puppy's reactions and willingness to either dive forward or withdraw, and never force him or her to interact with things they do not wish to interact with. Proceed at their pace by presenting the interaction and then observing their willingness to participate. Observing and learning their body language during this process will help you to deeply understand your dog's likes and dislikes. You will learn from their body language signals.

When strangers approach your pup do not allow them to automatically reach out and touch him, leave a little space and time for your puppy's reaction to be observed, and then you can grant or deny permission based upon you and your puppy's intuition. We all know that many people fail to ask permission before reaching for dogs that are strange to them, so it is your job to instruct strangers in the proper interaction process.

Socialization Summary Goals

1. Learning to remain calm when the world is buzzing around them.

2. Exposure in a safe manner to the environment that will encompass his or her world, including the rules and guidelines that accompany it.

3. Learning to respond to commands when they do not want to, for example, a dog in the midst of a chasing session with a fellow puppy, or while stalking an irresistible squirrel.

Let us begin by looking at how a puppy's social development process plays out from puppy to adulthood.

The first phase of socialization begins as early as 3 weeks and lasts to approximately 12 weeks, and during this time puppies discover that they are dogs and begin to play with their littermates. Survival techniques that they will use throughout their lives, such as biting, barking, chasing and fighting begin to be acted out.

Concurrently, during this period, puppies experience big changes socially and physically. Learning submissive postures and taking corrections from their mother along with interactions with their littermates teach them about hierarchies.

Keeping mother and puppies together for at least 8 weeks tends to increase their ability to get along well with other dogs and learn more about themselves and the consequences of their actions, such as the force of a bite on their brothers and sisters.

Between the ages of 7-12 weeks, a period of rapid learning occurs and they learn what humans are, and whether to accept them as safe. This is a crucial period, and has the greatest impact on all future social behavior.

This is the time we begin teaching puppies the acceptable rules of conduct. Take note that they have a short attention span and physical limitations. This is the easiest period to get your puppy comfortable with new things, and the chance to thwart negative behavioral issues that can stem from improper or incomplete socialization.

The sad reality is that behavioral problems are the greatest threat to the owner-dog relationship and the number one cause of death to dogs under 3 years of age. It is your responsibility to mentor your dog so a problem does not arise, and that shouldn't be difficult because you adore your pup and enjoy being in his company.

From birth, puppies should experience the handling and manipulation of their body parts, and be exposed to different people, places, situations, and other well-socialized animals. Encourage your puppy's exploring, curiosity and investigation of different environments. Games, toys, and a variety of surfaces and structures, such as rock, dirt, tile, concrete, pavement, tunnels and steps are all things to expose to your puppy.

This exposure should continue into adulthood and beyond. This aids in keeping your dog sociable instead of shy, and fearlessly capable of confronting different terrains.

It is important for your puppy to be comfortable playing, sleeping, or exploring alone. Schedule alone play with toys and solo naps in their crate or other safe areas that they enjoy. This teaches them to entertain themselves, and not become overly attached or have separation issues from their owners' absence. Getting them comfortable with their crate is also beneficial for travel and to use as their safe area.

Enrolling your puppy in classes before 3 months of age is an outstanding avenue to improve socialization, training and strengthening the bond between you and your puppy. You can begin socialization classes as early as 7-8 weeks. The recommendation is that your puppy has received at least 1 set of vaccines and a de-worming 7 days prior to starting the first class. At this time, puppies are still not out of harm's way from all diseases, but the risk is relatively low because of the primary vaccines, good care and the immunities provided by a mother's natural milk.

Keep a few things in mind when seeking play dates to help socialize your puppy. A stellar puppy class will have a safe, mature dog for the puppies to learn boundaries and other behaviors. When making play dates, puppies should be matched by personality and play styles.

Games such as retrieve or drop help to curb possessive behaviors as well as to help them learn to give up unsafe or off-limit items so that the item can be taken off them. Another important lesson during play is for puppies to learn to come back to their owner while engaged in a play session. Your dog should be willingly dependent on you and look to you for guidance.

Teach mature, easily stimulated dogs to relax before they are permitted to socialize with others. If you have an adult dog that enjoys flying solo, do not force him into situations. Teach your dogs and puppies to undertake less stimulating play and encourage passive play. This includes play that does not encompass dominance, mouthing or biting other puppies.

If you have rough play happening between multiple dogs or puppies, then interrupt the rough housing by frequently calling them to you and rewarding their attention, thus turning their attention to you. To dissuade mouthing contact, try to interject toys into the play. As they mature, overstimulating play can lead to aggression.

Two phases of fear imprinting occur in your growing puppy's life. A fear period is a stage during which your puppy may be more apt to perceive certain stimuli as threatening.

During these two periods, any event your puppy thinks is traumatic can have a lasting effect, possibly forever. The first period is from 8-11 weeks and the second is between 6-14 months of age. During these periods, you will want to keep your puppy clear of any frightening situations, but you will find that these are often difficult to determine.

A simple item like a chrome balloon on the floor could possibly scare the "bejeebers" out of your little pup. However, socialization continues and overcoming fears is part of that process so remain aware of what frightens your pup and slowly work at overcoming it.

There is no one-size-fits-all approach to know what your puppy will find fearful. Becoming familiar with canine body language can help you diagnose your pup's fears. The second period often reflects the dog becoming more reactive or apprehensive about new things. Larger breeds sometimes have an extended second period.

The Importance of Play

When observing dogs in a pack or family, one will notice that dogs and puppies often enjoy playing with each other. During play, puppies learn proper play etiquette, such as how hard to bite or mouth and the degree to play rough. Their mother and littermates provide feedback for them to learn.

Play is instinctual, and as a dog, behavior is something that needs to be satisfied. People and dogs both play throughout their lifetime and many studies show that this social interaction is important for mental and physical health.

Providing your dog with ample amounts of play through games, such as fetch, tug or chase helps to satisfy their need for play and assists in strengthening the bond between dog and owner. When guided in play, your dog will not only acquire the rules of play, but his physical and mental needs will also be met during the activity.

One terrific byproduct of play is that it burns off excess energy, and as a result, it helps keep negative behaviors from surfacing. Dogs are naturally full of energy and they need an outlet to avoid potential negative behaviors manifesting, such as chewing, digging and barking. While these behaviors serve them well in the wild, when living with humans they can be a detriment to the harmony and success of the relationship.

Socialization Summary

- Proper socialization requires patience, kindness and consistency during teaching. You and your dog should both have fun during this process. Allow your dog to proceed into new situations at his or her own pace, never force them into a situation in which they are not comfortable.

If you think that your dog may have a socialization issue, seek professional advice from a qualified behavioral professional. Because time is of the essence during their rapid growth period, do not delay.

- During the first few months of socialization, keep your puppy out of harm's way because he can easily pick up diseases from sniffing other dogs' feces and urine. When you are first exposing your puppy to new people, places or cars, it is good practice to carry him to and from the car. Follow this practice both inside and outside when near dog clinics.

Keeping your pup protected from contaminated ground surfaces will help keep him healthy until he has had vaccines and is a bit older. Avoid areas where you suspect other dogs might have eliminated.

- Socializing your puppy, especially before the age of six months, is a very important step in preventing future behavioral problems. I will add that it is necessary to save you a lot of future work.

- Socializing can and should continue throughout the lifetime of your dog. Socializing in a gentle and kind manner prevents aggressive and fearful behaviors, or those that would have possible litigious outcomes.

- A lack of socializing may lead to barking, shyness, destruction, territorialism or hyperactivity, and the risk of wearing Goth make-up and smoking clove cigarettes alone behind his doghouse.

The earlier you start socializing your pup, the better. However, all puppies and dogs can gradually be introduced into new and initially frightening situations, and will eventually learn to enjoy them. Canines can adapt to various and, sometimes, extreme situations, they just need your calm, guiding hand.

Don't fret if you are late in the game because you receive a 14-week-old puppy, you will still able to socialize them, but you might have a lot more work to do that can't be rushed.

- If your puppy does not engage with other dogs for months or years at a time, you can expect his behavior to be different when he encounters them again. I mean, how would you feel if your sixth-grade math teacher who you haven't seen in 17 years just walked up and sniffed you? This is why it is a lifelong process. Try to keep this in mind when you have those moments when you realize your dog hasn't been around construction work in ages and might need a reminder of the experience.

- This is also true when meeting new kinds of people, including, but not limited to, people wearing hats, folks with disabilities, people with facial hair, and people in local services, such as postal carriers, fire and police officers, and, of course, crowds of various types of people.

- Meeting new dogs is encouraged. Slowly expose your dog to other pets, such as cats, horses, birds, llamas, pigs, gerbils, lizards and all critters close to where you live. If they are used to seeing and smelling them, the familiarity will help to curtail sudden barking or chasing.

- Your dog's crate is not a jail. Be sure to take the time to teach your puppy to enjoy the comfort and privacy of his own crate. You want your dog's crate to be a place that he or she feels safe (for more information go to the crate-training chapter).

- To avoid doggy boredom, make sure your toy bin has plenty of toys for your puppy to choose. A Nylabone®, Kong® chew toys, ropes, balls and tugs are many of the popular things your dog can enjoy and their favorites should always be available for them wherever you have them sequestered.

Here are some methods you can use when exposing your dog to something new, or something of which he has previously been distrustful.

- Remain calm and upbeat. If he is leashed, keep it loose.

- Gradually expose him to the new stimulus and, if he is wary or fearful, never use force. Let him retreat if he needs to.

- Reward your dog using treats; give him a good scratch or an energetic run for being calm and exploring new situations. Additionally, add in vocal praise for accomplishments.

On a regular basis, expose your dog to the things in the world that he should be capable of coping with, which is everything. His gained familiarity will allow him to calmly deal with such situations in the future.

Stay away from routine, such as walking the same route daily. Though dogs love routine, periodically expose your dog to new locations and situations. This allows you to assess his need for further socialization and it allows you to discover new things. I certainly love exploring, so whenever possible I take my dogs to different areas for walks.

Socialization Checklist for Puppies and Adult Dogs

Be sure your dog is comfortable with the following:

- Male and female human adults.

- Male and female human children.

- Other household pets and dogs.

- Meeting strange dogs.

- Your house and neighborhood.

- Mechanical noises, such as lawn mowers and vehicles.

- Special circumstance people, for example, those in wheelchairs, using crutches, wearing braces, with Tourette syndrome or even strange indefinable cousin Larry who walks with a limp.

To ensure that your dog is not selfish, make sure that he or she is comfortable sharing the following:

- His food bowl, toys, and bedding, and that those can all be touched by you and others without receiving aggression from your dog.

- The immediate space shared with strangers, especially with children. This is necessary for your puppy's socialization so that he does not get paranoid or freak out in small places, e.g. at the next-door neighbor's house or in an elevator.

- His best friend you, and all family members and friends, and is not overprotective or territorial towards others.

For road tripping with your dog, make sure he or she is:

- Comfortable in all types of vehicles, such as a car, truck, minivan, SUV and, if applicable, public transportation.

- Always properly and safely restrained.

- Comfortable by regularly stopping for elimination breaks and to drink fluids.

- Knowledgeable about how to operate a stick shift as well as an automatic and wears eye protection if he is letting the wind pound his face.

I have faith that you will do a terrific job in socializing your dog so that he can greet the world calmly and is able to enjoy the surprises it regularly delivers.

4 Navigating Problem Behaviors

"I am in favor of animal rights as well as human rights. That is the way of a whole human being." — Abraham Lincoln

How to deal with a problem behavior before it becomes a habit

Everyone likes his or her own space to feel comfortable, familiar and safe, and your dog is no different. A proper living area is a key factor to avoiding all kinds of potential problems. Think of all the things your puppy will encounter during his life with humans, such as appliances and mechanical noises that are not common in nature, and can be frightening to your dog. It is essential to use treats, toys and praise to assist you and your dog while in the midst of training and socializing.

Dogs are social creatures and it is essential to communicate with them. Communication is always the key to behavior reinforcement. Regularly rewarding calm behavior and showing that you control his favorite things acts as a pathway to thwarting problems that can surface later.

21

Keep your Mini Aussie's world happy. Make sure it is getting a proper amount of exercise and that he is being challenged mentally. Make sure he is receiving enough time in the company of other dogs and other people. Keep a close eye on his diet, offering him good, healthy, dog-appropriate foods. Avoid excessive helpings when treating him.

It is important that you are a strong leader. Dogs are pack animals and your dog needs to know that you are the leader. Do not let situations become questionable scenarios in which your dog is uncertain about who is in charge. Your puppy will feel confident and strong if he works for his rewards and knows that he or she has a strong, confident leader to follow. Let your dog show you good behavior before you provide him with rewards.

Your dog's first step towards overcoming the challenges in life is in understanding what motivates his behavior. Some behaviors your dog will exhibit are instinctual. Chewing, barking, digging, jumping, chasing and leash pulling are things that all dogs do because it is in their genetic make-up. These natural behaviors differ from the ones we have inadvertently trained into the domestic canine.

Behaviors, such as nudging our hands to be petted or barking for attention are actually accidently reinforced by people and are not innate and should never be rewarded.

What motivates your dog to do what he does or does not do? You may wonder why he does not come when you call him while he is playing with other dogs. Simply, this may be because coming to you is far less exciting than scrapping with the same species. When calling your dog, you can change this behavior by offering him a highly coveted treat and, after treating him, allow him to continue playing for a while.

Start this training aspect slowly, and in short distances from where he is playing. Gradually increase the distances and distractions when you beckon your dog. After he is coming regularly to you, then begin to treat him less frequently and supplement it with verbal or physical praise.

Here are some helpful tips to use when trying to help your Mini Australian Shepherd through challenging behavior.

- Are you accidentally rewarding bad behavior? Remember that your dog may see any response from you as a reward. You can ignore the bad behavior if you are patient enough, or you can give your puppy the equivalent of a human time out for a few minutes. Make sure the time out environment is a calm, quiet and safe place, but a very dull place that is not his crate.

- Think about the quality of his diet and health. Is your dog getting enough playtime, mental and physical exercise, and sleep? Is this a medical problem? Do not ignore the range of possibilities that could be eliciting your dog's challenging behavior. An unseen physical or mental deformity or ailment could be the cause of a chronic negative behavior.

- Be sure and practice replacement behavior. Reward him with something that is much more appealing than the perceived reward that he is getting when he is acting in an undesirable manner. It is important to reward his good behavior before he misbehaves. If done consistently and correctly, this will reinforce good behaviors, and reduce poor behaviors.

For example, in the hopes of receiving love, your dog is repeatedly nudging your hand; instead teach him to sit by only giving him love after he sits, and never if he nudges you. If you command, "Sit", and he complies, and then you pat him on the head or speak nicely to him, or both, your dog will associate compliance with sitting with nice things.

If your pooch nudges you and you turn away and never acknowledge him, he will understand that behavior is not associated with nice things. In a scenario where your dog is continually nudging you for attention, catch him before he comes running into your room and begins nudging you. When you see him approaching, immediately say, "Sit", to stop him in his tracks.

- While practicing the replacement behavior, be sure you reward the right response and ignore the mistakes. Remember, any response to the wrong action could be mistaken as a reward by your dog, so try to remain neutral when you ignore him, which includes visual, touch and verbal acknowledgement. Be sure to offer your dog a greater reward for the correct action than the joy he is getting from doing the wrong action.

- Your dog's bad behavior may be caused by something that makes him fearful. If you decipher this as the problem, then change his mind about what he perceives frightening. Pair the scary thing with something he loves. For example, your dog has a problem with the local skateboarder. Pair the skateboarder's visit with a delicious treat and lots of attention. He will soon look forward to the daily arrival of the skateboarder.

- Always, remain patient with your dog and do not force changes. Work gradually and slowly. Forcing behavioral changes on your dog may lead to worsening the unwanted behavior. Training requires that you work as hard as your dog, and maybe harder, because you have to hone your observational skills, intuition, timing, patience, laughter and the understanding of your dog's body language and demeanor.

5 Rewarding Instead of Punishing

"In order to really enjoy a dog, one doesn't merely try to train him to be semi-human. The point of it is to open oneself to the possibility of becoming partly a dog." ~Edward Hoagland

It is always better to reward your Mini Aussie instead of punishing him or her. Here are a few reasons why:

- If you punish your dog, it can make him distrust, avoid or fear you, or make him aggressive. If you rub your dog's nose in his poop or pee, he may avoid going to the bathroom in front of you. This is going to make his public life difficult.

- Physical punishment has the tendency to escalate in severity. If you get your dog's attention by a light tap on the nose, he will soon get used to that and ignore it. Shortly the contact will become more and more violent. As we know, violence is not the answer.

- Punishing your dog may have some bad side effects. For example, if you are using a pinch collar, it may tighten when he encounters other dogs. Dogs are very smart, but they are not always logical. When your dog encounters another dog, the pinching of the collar may lead him to thinking erroneously that the other dog is the reason for the pinch. Pinch collars have been linked to the reinforcement of aggressive behaviors in dogs.

- Electric fences will make him avoid the yard.

- Choke collars can cause injuries to a dog's throat as well as cause back and neck misalignment.

- You may inadvertently develop an adversarial relationship with your dog if you punish him instead of working through a reward system and correctly leading him. If you only look for the mistakes within your dog, this is all you will ever see. In your mind, you will see a problem dog. In your dog's mind, he will see his master's anger and distrust.

- You ultimately want to shape your dog's incorrect actions into acceptable actions. By punishing your dog, he will learn only to avoid punishment. He is not learning to change the behavior you want changed, instead he learns to be sneaky or to do the very minimum to avoid being punished. Your dog can become withdrawn and seemingly inactive. Permanent psychological damage can be done if a dog lives in fear of punishment.

- If you punish rather than reward neither you nor your dog will be having a very good time. It will be a constant, sometimes painful struggle. If you have children, they will not be able to participate in a punishment-based training process because it is too difficult and truly no fun.

- Simply put, if you train your dog using rewards, you and your dog will have more fun and form a better relationship. Rely on rewards to change his behavior by using treats, toys, playing, petting, affection or anything else you know your dog likes.

If your dog is doing something that you do not like, replace the habit with another by teaching your dog to do something different and then rewarding him or her for doing the replacement action. Then everyone can enjoy the outcome.

6 Clicker Training Your Mini Aussie

You can choose not to clicker train your dog and use this book's reward-based training techniques without a clicker, however clicker training is proven to speed up puppy and dog training.

What the heck is that clicking noise? Well, it's a clicker, thus the name. If you are a product of a Catholic school, you might be very familiar with this device. You probably have nightmares of large, penguin-like women clicking their way through your young life. Yes, it was annoying and at times terrifying, however, when it comes to training your dog, it will be helpful and fun.

A clicker is a small device that makes a sound that is easily distinguishable and is not commonly heard in nature, or is it one that humans normally produce. This unique sound keeps the dog that is being trained from becoming confused by accidently hearing a word used in conversation or another environmental noise. You click at the exact time when your dog does the correct action and then immediately follow the click with a treat or reward.

The clicker is used to inform your dog that he did the right thing and that a treat is coming. When your dog does the right thing after you command, like drop your Chanel purse that is dangling from his mouth, you click and reward him with a nice treat.

Using the clicker system allows you to set your puppy up to succeed while you ignore or make efforts to prevent bad behavior. It is a very positive, humane system and punishment is not part of the process.

Here are some questions often asked about clicker training:

- "Do you need to have the clicker on your person at all times?" No.

The clicker is a teaching device. Once your dog understands what you want him to do, you can then utilize verbal or hand cues, and if inclined verbal praise or affection instead of clicking and treating.

- "Can rewards be other things besides treats?" Sure.

Actually, you should mix it up. Use the clicker and a treat when you first start teaching. When your puppy has learned the behavior you want, then switch to other rewards, such as petting, play, toys or lottery tickets. Remember always to ask for the wanted target behavior, such as sit, stay or come, before you reward your dog. These verbal reinforcements can augment the clicker training and reward giving.

- "With all these treats, isn't my dog going to get fat?" No.

If you figure treats into your dog's daily intake and subtract from meals accordingly, your dog will be fine. The treats should be as small as a corn kernel, just a taste. Use food from his regular meals when you are training indoors, but when outdoors, use fresh treats like meat or cheese.

There are many distractions outside and a tasty fresh treat will help keep your puppy's attention. Dogs' finely honed senses will smell even the smallest of treats and this keeps them attentive.

- "What do I do if my dog doesn't act out the command?"

Simple, if your dog disobeys you, it is because he has not been properly trained yet. Do not C/T (click and treat), or verbally praise him for any wrong actions, instead ignore the wrong action. Continue training because your dog has not yet learned the command and action you are teaching him to perform. He, after all, is just a dog.

If he is disobeying, he has been improperly or incompletely trained, or perhaps the treats are not tasty enough. Try simplifying the task and attempt to make the reward equal to or better than what is distracting your dog. Eventually your dog will understand what action should be performed when the command word is spoken.

Helpful Hint

- Conceal the treat! Do NOT show your dog the treat before pressing the clicker and making the clicking sound. If you do this, he will be responding to the treat and not the click and this will undermine your training strategy.

Why and How Clicker Training Works

The important reason I put this information together is that it is essential to understand why timing and consistency is important, and why clicker training works. If any of this is confusing, do not worry, because I walk you through the training process step-by-step.

Clicker training started over 70 years ago and has become a tried and true method for training dogs and other animals. The outcome of using a clicker is an example of conditioned reinforcement. Rewarding the animal in combination with clicker use has proven highly effective as a positive reinforcement training method. It is a humane and effective way of training dogs without instilling fear for non-compliance.

In the 1950s, Keller Breland, a pioneer in animal training, used a clicker while training many different species of animal, including marine mammals. He experienced great success using this method to train these animals. The system he developed for clicker training marine mammals is still in use today.

Keller also trained dogs using the clicker. Because of its effectiveness, it was brought into use by others in the dog training community. Gradually, clicker training for dogs gained more and more popularity and by the early 1980s its use became widespread. The success of the clicker spans 7 decades and now is a widely accepted standard for dog training. Millions of dogs worldwide have been successfully trained using a clicker.

A trainer will use the clicker to mark desired actions as they occur. At the exact instant the animal performs the desired action, the trainer clicks and promptly delivers a food reward or other type of positive reinforcement. One key to clicker training is a trainer's timing, and timing is crucial.

For example, clicking and rewarding slightly too early or too late will reinforce the action that is occurring at that very instant rather than the action you were targeting the reward for. The saying goes, "You get what you click for".

To improve your ability using a clicker, I recommend reading one of Karen Pryor's books on clicker training, such as the latest edition of "Getting Started: Clicker Training for Dogs".

Shaping – Super important for clicker training success.

Clicker trainers often use the process of shaping. Shaping is the process of the gradual transformation of a specific action into the desired action by rewarding each successive progression towards the desired action. This is done by gradually molding or training the dog to perform a specific response by first reinforcing the small, successive responses that are similar to the desired response, instead of waiting for the perfect outcome to occur.

The trainer looks for small progressions that are heading in the direction towards the total completion of the desired action and then clicks and treats. It is important to recognize and reward those tiny steps that are made in the target direction. During training, the objective is to create opportunities for your dog to earn frequent rewards.

In the beginning, it is acceptable to increase the frequency of C/T to every 3-4 seconds or less. By gauging the dog's abilities and improvements, the trainer can gradually increase the length of time between a C/T. It is necessary to assess the dog's progress from moment to moment, adjusting the C/T frequency to achieve the desired outcome.

During training, and in conjunction with clicker use, the introduction of a cue word or hand signal can be applied. Eventually, the clicker can be phased out in favor of a cue or cues that have been reinforced during the training sessions. As a result, your dog will immediately respond by reacting, obeying and performing actions to your hand gestures and verbal commands.

Watching this unfold is a highly satisfying process that empowers your friend to be the best he can be.

Why is clicking effective over using a word cue first?

The clicking sound is a unique sound that is not found in nature, and it is more precise than a verbal command. Verbal commands can be confusing because the human voice has many tonal variations, whereas the clicker consistently makes a sound that your dog will not confuse with any other noise. It is also effective because it is directed at your pup and followed by good things. Therefore, your dog completely understands which action is preferred and your dog will quickly understand that the click is followed by a reward.

The click sound is produced in a quick and accurate way that is in response to the slightest action that your dog performs. The clarity offered by this tool increases the bond between you and your dog and results in making your dog more interested in the training sessions, and ultimately your relationship becomes more engaging and entertaining. Dare I say fun?

On that note, do not forget to always have fun and add variety to your training sessions. Variety is the spice of life, mix up those treats, rewards and commands for each training session.

Clicker training works this way

At the exact instant the action occurs, the trainer should click. If a dog begins to sit, the trainer recognizes that and at the exact moment the dog's buttocks hit the ground the trainer clicks and offers the dog a reward. Usually the reward is a small kernel-sized food treat, but a reward can be a toy, play or affection. Whatever the dog enjoys is a reward worth giving.

Sometimes, after as little as 2-3 clicks have been issued a dog will associate the sound of the click with something it enjoys. Once the association is made, it will repeat the action it did when hearing the click and receiving the reward. Click = Reward. When this goes off in the dog's head, repeating the action makes sense.

The 3 steps are as follows:

1. Get the action you request

2. Mark the action with your clicker

3. Reinforce the action with a reward

How do you ask for actions when clicker training your dog?

During clicker training, before adding a cue command such as stay, you wait until your dog completely understands the action. A cue is the name of the action, e.g. sit, stay or come, or it can be a hand signal that you are using when you ask your dog to perform a specific action. Your dog should know the action stay from the click and reward before you verbally name it. He or she has connected remaining in the same place to receiving a click and reward.

When training you do not want to add the cue until your dog has been clicked 5-10 times for the action, and is accurately responding in a manner that clearly shows he understands which action earns the click and reward. This is called introducing the cue.

Teaching your dog the name of the cue or action requires saying or signaling before your dog repeats the action. After several repetitions, begin to click and reward when your dog performs the action, and be sure the cue is given before the reward. Your dog will learn to listen and watch for the cue, knowing that if he performs the action a reward will follow.

Clicker Training Help

If your dog is not obeying the cue, answer the following questions and then revise your training process so that your dog knows the meaning of the clicker sound cue during all situations. Importantly, be sure that your dog is and feels rewarded for performing the correct action.

Trainers never assume a dog is intentionally disobeying them without asking the questions below.

1. Does your dog understand the meaning of the cue?

2. Does your dog understand the meaning of the cue in the situation that it was first taught, but not in the different situations in which you gave the cue?

3. Is the reward for performing the action satisfying your dog's needs? Is the treat or toy worth the effort?

Once you have answered these questions, change your training process to be certain that your dog understands the cue in all situations, including highly distracting situations in a busy park.

Then be sure your dog is adequately rewarded and that it is clear your dog feels that he or she has been properly rewarded. This will help put you both back on the path of mutual understanding during your training sessions.

This will become clearer as you read about how to teach commands.

7 Dog Treats

You are training your puppy and it is going well because your pup is the best dog in the world. Oh yes he is, everyone knows this to be true. Because of this fact, you want to make sure that you are giving your dog the right types of treat.

Treats are easy as long as you stay away from the things that aren't good for dogs, such as avocados, onions, garlic, coffee, tea, caffeinated drinks, grapes, raisins, macadamia nuts, peaches, plums, fruit pits, seeds, persimmons and chocolates.

Dog owners can make treats from many different foods. Treats should always be sized about the dimension of a kernel of corn. This makes them easy to grab from treat pouches and still flavorful enough for your hound to desire them.

All a dog needs is a little taste to keep him interested. The kernel size is something that is swiftly eaten and swallowed, thus not distracting him from the training session. A treat is only to provide a quick taste, used for enticement and reinforcement, not as a snack or meal.

When you are outdoors and there are many distractions, treats should be of a higher quality and coveted by your pooch. Trainers call it a higher value treat because it is worth your dog breaking away from the activity they are engaged in. Perhaps cubes of cheese or dried and cooked meats will qualify as your dog's high value treat.

Make sure you mix up the types of treat by keeping a variety of treats available. Nothing is worse during training than when your puppy turns his nose up at a treat because he has grown bored of it or holds it to be of lesser value than his interests hold.

Types of Treats

Human foods that are safe for dogs include most fruits and veggies, cut up meats that are raw or cooked, yogurt, peanut butter, kibble, and whatever else you discover that your dog likes. Be sure that it is good for them, in particular their digestive system. Be advised that not all human foods are good for dogs. Please read about human foods that are acceptable for dogs and observe your dog's stools when introducing new treats.

How many times have you heard a friend or family member tell you about some crazy food that their dog loves? Dogs do love a massive variety of foods; unfortunately, not all of the foods that they think they want to eat are good for them. Dog treating is not rocket science but it does take a little research, common sense and paying attention to how your dog reacts after wolfing down a treat.

Many people like to make homemade treats and that is okay, just keep to the rules I just mentioned and watch what you are adding while having fun in the kitchen. Remember to research and read the list of vegetables dogs can and cannot eat, and understand that pits and seeds can cause choking and intestinal issues such as the dreaded doggy flatulence.

When preparing treats, first remove any seeds and pits, and clean all fruits and veggies before slicing them into doggie-size treats.

Before purchasing treats, look at the ingredients on the packaging and be sure there are no chemicals, fillers, additives, colors and things that are unhealthy. Some human foods that are tasty to us might not be so tasty to your dog and he will let you know. Almost all dogs love some type of raw or cooked meats. In tiny nibble sizes, these treats work great at directing their attention where you want it focused. In a highly distracting area, a piece of liver might be exactly what you need to keep your dog's focus.

Here are some treat ideas:

- Whole grain cereals like cheerios without added sugar are a good choice.

- Kibble (dry foods). Put some in a paper bag and boost the aroma factor by tossing in some bacon or another meat product. Dogs are all about those yummy aromas.

- Beef jerky that has no pepper or heavy seasoning added.

- Carrots, and apple pieces, and some dogs even enjoy melons.

- Meats that have been cubed and are not highly processed or salted, these are easy to make at home as well. You can use cooked leftover foods.

- Shredded cheese, string cheese or cubed cheese. Dogs love cheese!

- Cream cheese, peanut butter or spray cheese. Give your dog a small dollop to lick for every proper behavior. These work well when training puppies to ring a bell when they need to go outside for elimination.

- Baby food meat products, they certainly don't look yummy to us but dogs adore them.

- Ice cubes, but if your dog has dental problems, proceed cautiously.

- Commercial dog treats, but use caution, there are loads of them on the market. Look for those that do not have preservatives, byproducts, or artificial colors. Additionally, take into consideration the country of origin.

Never feed or treat your four-legged friend from the dining table, because you do not want to teach that begging actions are acceptable. When treating, give treats far from the dinner table or from areas where people normally gather to eat such as by the BBQ.

Time to Treat

The best time to issue dog treats is between meals. Treating soon after a mealtime makes all treats less effective, so remember this when planning your training sessions. If during training you need to refocus your dog back on the training session, keep a high value treat in reserve.

Obviously, if your dog is full from mealtime he will be less likely to want a treat reward than if he is slightly hungry. If your dog is not hungry, your training sessions will likely be more difficult and far less effective. This is why it is a good idea to reward correct actions with praise, play or toys, and not rely exclusively on treats.

- Love and attention are considered rewards and are certainly positive reinforcement that can be just as effective as an edible treat. Dog treating comprises edibles, praise and attention. Engaging in play or allowing some quality time with their favorite rope toy is also effective and, at times, these rewards are crucial to dog training.

- Do not give your dog a treat without asking for an action first. Say, "Sit", and after your dog complies, deliver the treat. This reinforces your training and their obedience.

- Avoid treating your dog when he is overstimulated and running amuck in an unfocused state of mind. This can be counterproductive and might reinforce a negative behavior, resulting in the inability to get your dog's attention.

- Due to their keen sense of smell, they will know long before you could ever know that there is a tasty snack nearby, but keep it out of sight. Issue your command and wait for your dog to obey before presenting the reward. Remember when dog treating, it is important to be patient and loving, but it is equally important not to give the treat until your dog obeys.

- Some dogs have a natural gentleness to them and always take from your hand gently, while other dogs need some guidance to achieve this.

If your dog is a bit rough during treat grabbing, go ahead and train the command, "Gentle!" when giving treats. Be firm from this point forward. Give no treats unless they are gently taken from your hand. Remain steadfast with your decision to implement this, and soon your pup will comply if he wants the tasty treat.

Bribery vs. Reward Dog Treating

The other day a friend of mine mentioned bribing for an action that he had commanded. I thought about it later and thought I would clarify for my readers. Bribery is the act of offering the food visually in advance so that the dog will act out a command or alter a behavior. Reward is giving your dog his favorite toy, treat, love or affection after he has performed the commanded action.

An example of bribery can happen when you want your dog to come, and before you call your dog, you hold a cube of steak for them to see. Reward would be giving your dog the steak after they have obeyed the come command. Never show the treats before issuing commands.

Bribed dogs learn to comply with your wishes only when they see food. The rewarded dog realizes that they only receive rewards after performing the desired actions. This is also assisted by introducing non-food items as rewards when training and treating.

8 Chewing Stuff

All puppies love and enjoy chewing, especially while teething, but a chewing Mini Aussie can do some serious damage, so be alert and diligent to thwart that behavior so it does not get out of hand. Keep many toys and doggy chews around so that you can redirect your puppy towards the dog-specific toys instead of your new black leather shoes.

Let your pup know that his or her toys are the only acceptable items to be chewed. Loneliness, boredom, fear, teething and separation anxiety are feelings that can motivate your puppy to chew.

Until you have trained that chewing only happens with their dog toys, while you are away you should probably leave your pup in his crate or gated area. At all times be sure to throw some dog chew toys in their crate, limiting your pup's chewing to only those indestructible natural rubber chew toys.

Lots of physical exercise, training, and mental challenges will assist in steering your dog away from destructive chewing. Until your puppy is over his "I'll chew anything phase", hide your shoes and other items that you do not want chewed. Before you bring your new puppy home, all areas where they will have access to need to be properly puppy-proofed. This protects your possessions and the pup's life.

Puppy proofing your home entails removing all harmful items that a puppy might chew or swallow, which, unfortunately, means everything. Puppies love to put anything into their mouths. After all, they are kids learning about the world. It will be necessary to elevate electrical cords, remove floor debris, and all other random objects that a puppy can chew, eat or swallow.

Thoroughly inspect your entire house that is accessible to your puppy. Apply bitter spray to appropriate furniture and fixed objects that require protection. Take extra caution to remove from the puppy's reach all chemicals, pharmaceuticals and toxic liquids that might be accessible around the house.

The "Leave it!" and "Drop it!" commands should be trained early so that you can quickly steer your pup away from anything that is not his to chew. Avoid letting your dog mouth or chew on your fingers or hand, because that can lead to biting behaviors that can cause many problems for you and them.

Teething

Between the third and sixth week your puppy will begin to feel the notorious baby teeth eruption. Puppy teeth are not designed to grind heavy foods, and consist of predominantly small, razor sharp canines and incisors. These new teeth number about 28, and during this painful and frustrating teething period, puppies will attempt to seek relief on anything within reach that they can clamp their little mouths around.

Later, when the baby teeth fall out and their adult teeth emerge, this will again cause discomfort, further increasing their drive to chew in search of relief. Usually after 6 months, the intense chewing phase begins to wane. Although some variance exists by breed, adult dogs have 42 teeth with the molars coming in last at around 6 to 7 months of age.

Puppies are motivated to chew because of the discomfort that comes from teething, as well as to investigate new objects of interest. Chewing is a normal dog behavior that can be steered and directed toward owner-approved toys and objects.

Dogs certainly love to chew on bones, and they can spend hours gnawing until they feel that they have successfully scoured it clean, sometimes burying it for a later chew session, or solely as a trophy. Wood, bones and toys are some of the objects that occupy a dog during the activity of chewing.

Chewing not only provides stimulation and fun, but it serves to reduce a dog's anxiety. It is our job to identify what our puppies can and cannot chew on, while gently establishing and enforcing the rules of chewing. This process begins by providing an ample amount of safe chew toys for your puppy.

Chew toys

A non-edible chew toy is an object made for dogs to chew that is neither consumable nor destructible. Non-food items eaten by dogs are dangerous and can sometimes seriously harm your dog, so it is imperative to provide high quality and durable chew toys.

Choosing the type of chew toy will depend upon your dog's individual preferences and chewing ability, so you may have to go through several to find the most appropriate. Some super chewer dogs can destroy a rawhide chew in a fraction of the time it takes other dogs, so your pup's prowess and jaw power will dictate the type of chew that you will want to provide.

Edible chews such as pig ears, rawhide bones, Nylabones® and other natural chew products are also available and appropriate for your puppy or adult dog. Beware that sometimes edibles can come apart in large chunks or pieces, thus having the potential to be swallowed, or possibly choke a dog.

For safety, keep an eye on your dog whenever he is working away on an edible chew. While your puppy is discovering the joy of chewing, take notice of the chews that he enjoys most.

KONG® and Petsafe® make plenty of top quality chew toys, including those that can be stuffed with food, such as kibble or cheese, that hold your dog's interest. KONG® products as well as the Petsafe® Busy Buddy® line are made from natural rubber and have a stellar reputation for durability.

Many other brands are available too. When choosing chew toys, take into consideration whether or not you are purchasing a natural or synthetic product, as well as keep in mind what your pal's preferences are. Usually, anything that you stuff with food will have a puppy craving that particular toy, but be aware that that is not always the case.

Stuffing Chew Toys

There are some basic guidelines to follow when using a 'stuffable' chew toy. First, kibble is the recommended foodstuff when filling your puppy's chew toy. Kibble assists in keeping your puppy at a normal weight, and if this is a concern, you can simply exclude the amount you used in the toy from his normal feeding portion. Secondly, you can use tastier treats, such as cooked meat or freeze-dried liver, but these should be reserved for special rewards. There are plenty of stuffing recipes available, but be cautious about the frequency you treat your puppy with special stuffing.

Be conscious of when you reward your puppy, and avoid doing so when bad behaviors are exhibited. For example, if your puppy has been incessantly barking all afternoon, if you provide a stuffed chew toy do not reward him with something utterly delectable.

The art to stuffing chew toys is that the toy holds your puppy's interest, and keeps him occupied. For your success, you will want to stuff the toy in a way that a small portion of food comes out easily, thus quickly rewarding your puppy. After this initial jackpot, the goal is to keep your puppy chewing while gradually being rewarded with small bits of food that he actively extracts. You can use a high value treat, such as a piece of meat stuffed deeply into the smallest hole that will keep your dog occupied for hours in search of the prized morsel.

With a little creativity and practice, the art of chew-toy stuffing will be acquired, benefitting you and your canine friend. After trial and error, you will begin to understand what fillings and arrangements will keep your puppy occupied for longer and longer periods.

Why Feed Dinner from Stuffed Chew Toys?

Here is some advice that I gleaned off a friend of mine, and it does seem to pack some merit. As you are probably aware, the current practice indicates that puppies should be fed 2 to 3 times daily, from their bowl. There is nothing wrong with this, but it does raise a question as to whether perhaps they think that they are being rewarded for the unacceptable behavior that was possibly acted just prior to feeding time. *This should be taken into consideration, and feeding should be adjusted to avoid potential negative behavior reinforcement.

The other item that I was made aware of is that if you feed your puppy by stuffing his chew toy, it will occupy more of his time and keep him from acting negatively due to boredom, excessive curiosity or abundant adrenal stores.

The argument against bowl feeding is that it supplants the activity of searching for food as they would in the wild, and as a result of the quick gratification of the easy meal, there remains an over-abundance of time remaining to satisfy the dog's mental and physical stimulation.

To understand this better you have to put yourself into a puppy's paws. Besides sleeping and training, your dog has about 12 hours each day to fill with satisfying and rewarding activity. Resulting from an excess of unoccupied time, normal behaviors, such as grooming, barking, chewing, walking and playing can become repetitive and unfulfilling.

Sometimes an activity can lose its initial purpose and meaning, only to become a way to pass time instead of serving as a positive function of daily life. Obsessive and compulsive behaviors can come out of these long sessions of boredom. For example, vocalizing for alarm can become ceaseless barking, and grooming can turn into excessive licking or scratching likely resulting in harm to the skin.

It falls upon us to instruct our puppies about healthy, calm and relaxing ways to pass the time of day. This is a critical part of training and socialization. Remember, that by stuffing the chew toy full of kibble you can successfully occupy hours of your puppy's time, helping to reduce the possibility of negative behaviors overtaking your puppy.

This can be accomplished by redirecting his attention to an activity that he enjoys, keeping his mind distracted to avoid loneliness and boredom. Because his time is spent chewing the approved toy, he is kept calm and his time occupied, and this along with periodically rewarding him with bits of kibble, will thus reduce the possibility of him developing any of the potential, aforementioned negative behaviors.

This feeding option is a method originally suggested by Dr. Ian Dunbar, a famed reward-based trainer and SIRIUS® puppy-training pioneer. However, this method is not essential to maintain and train a healthy puppy; I felt it was worth mentioning since I was writing about chew toys.

Many people refrain from feeding their dogs kibble, utilizing the optional diet of raw foods, thus a modification to the feeding method would be required here. Other factors when utilizing this method should be your dog's individual personality, as well as his ability to withdraw food from the toy. Whichever feeding method you choose to use, be certain to feed your puppy the healthiest, least processed, non-chemical laden foods that you can find.

Chew Toy Training

This is an option for controlling and shaping the chewing behavior. Something that I learned from other trainers is how to establish a chew-toy obsession for your puppy. When you bring your puppy home, you should immediately begin exposing him to chew toys, always keeping them in close proximity, so you can effectively steer all of his chewing urges to these toys instead of your expensive leather shoes, flip-flops, or comfy slippers.

Puppies love to chew on just about anything that they can get their mouths on, but depending upon your puppy's personality, variance exists in the frequency and ferocity of the chewing. There is no reason to leave it to chance. By establishing an early obsession with chew toys, you can be assured that all of your valuable human articles will be spared from the chewing machines we call puppies. Until he has completely learned that his toys are the only acceptable objects for him to chew, everything in your house should be considered at risk.

Chew toys provide puppies with a focal point in which to channel their energy, and serve to keep boredom from setting up shop. It is a necessity to teach your puppy early on that the chew toys you provide are fun and delicious. A good way to do this is to take advantage of the hollow toys and stuff them with kibble, or other tasty treats of your choice.

To bolster this training, you can keep your puppy's food bowl hidden for the first few weeks after his arrival, and serve all of your puppy's kibble in the stuffed toy, or a sterilized bone. Taking this action will support your puppy's quick understanding and connection between good things and his chew toys. Remember, the goal here is to create an obsession with chew toys, resulting in a dog that will leave all of the other non-chew toy items alone.

In order to reinforce his chew-toy obsession, you can use what is called the confinement program. Through a process in which you narrow the choices of items your dog has available to chew, your puppy eventually will find a kind of solace in his own chew toys. His association with his own chew toys will grow as he grows, ultimately resulting in him craving to chew only his chew toys and nothing else.

The confinement program training begins by securing your puppy behind his gated area and providing him with plenty of chew toys to occupy his alone time. Whether you do this prior to leaving the house or while you are in the house, do not forget to leave fresh water for your puppy. Additionally, every hour when you let your puppy out for elimination, begin to introduce chew-toy games.

There are a variety of games you can play, such as find the hidden chew toy, chew toy tug-o-war and fetch. These games will reinforce his attachment to his chew toys, and help create a positive attitude toward them. By providing your puppy with a singular choice that is stuffed with food, he will eventually develop a strong chew-toy obsession.

After your dog has formed his chew-toy habit, and has not had any other chewing mishaps, you can broaden his world by expanding his available confinement space to two rooms. As he proves his compliance by not chewing items beyond his chew toys, you can expand his roaming range to other rooms in the house, while gradually working up his access to the entire house.

If your puppy makes a chewing mistake, then return him to confinement for 3-6 weeks, depending upon his progress and the success of further confinement training. After a 3-week period, you will want to test the results of the behavioral modifications resulting from his confinement program (limited areas to roam).

Grant him more access and see if your puppy has reverted to chewing objects on your no chew list, or if the program has been a success and it is time to move on and enlarge his range. If he reverts again to chewing on objects other than his chew toys, continue the confinement program for a couple of more weeks then test him again.

Because this training will concurrently run parallel with housetraining, you will also need to monitor when your puppy is having house-soiling accidents. Because your puppy is having accidents indoors, this may limit the house access that you can provide your puppy. It is recommended that in order for you to begin expanding his indoor range of access, your dog should be successfully housetrained and beyond the possibility of a soiling accident. *This training should not conflict with your housetraining.

The benefits of making your dog's chew toys an obsession are more than just for preventing household destruction. It also reduces barking and keeps him from running around the house, because while your puppy is chewing he is distracted, and thus unable to perform other activities.

Another potential behavior issue that has negative implications is the separation anxiety that can occur because of your absence. Because chewing occupies your puppy's down time, it helps to prevent the development of separation anxiety while you are away. It acts like a blanket or a teddy bear to a child.

Furthermore, it is pointed out that a chew-toy addiction is good for dogs that have obsessive compulsive disorder. This addiction offers them an acceptable avenue to work out their obsessive compulsions. It is not a cure but instead a therapeutic device that can be used by them.

"Is this a good obsession for my puppy?"

Yes, it is and, additionally, a good habit that is difficult to break. The benefits are that your puppy will not be chewing your personal items, and it works well towards preventing him developing compulsive behaviors, such as barking, digging, and howling, as well as feelings such as anxiety from being alone, along with a list of other undesirable behaviors.

The action of chewing also has a calming benefit, thus acts as a stress reliever. It turns out that a simple rubber chew toy is an effective tool for controlling and shaping behaviors, as well as a therapeutic tool to occupy and soothe.

PART II
Schooling Begins

9 Effective Mini Aussie Training

I have seen some Mini Aussies that spend a lot of time cuddling with their humans where as others only enjoy the occasional hello and show of affection. This depends upon your dog and your own personality. There are no absolutes in dog breed profiles; they are just an average based upon how the standard reads and what breeders try to attain for their Mini Aussie puppies. However, it is more common for Mini Aussies to pine to be near the family than apart and appreciate the family camaraderie.

Part of good training is learning your dog's personality, likes, dislikes and reactions to your actions. Dogs are amazingly tuned to every facial tick and physical action us humans do, so remember in your dog's presence to be aware of what you are doing. This is often forgotten by individuals who are in the process of shaping their dogs behavior.

Training is always happening when your dog is around, and the first year is when you establish your dog's behavioral foundation. The first few months are crucial for you to be active and present in your dog's life, assisting them in knowing what it acceptable and regularly training your dog the basic obedience commands and appropriate behaviors.

Puppies learn very quickly, which is one of the reasons why we begin training at 6-8 weeks of age. This is because they are curious and unencumbered with any previous memories that are either good or bad.

Because of this, I stress making training enjoyable and fun, they don't know or think of it as work or negative unless you make it negative. Refraining from harsh vocal tones and physical actions works well and keeps fear or anxiety from creeping into what is supposed to be a fun time for bonding with your new best furry friend. Believe me, there will be plenty of laughs and head shaking moments during training.

To maintain your place in the family hierarchy, your new little furry friend must know that it is unacceptable to be aggressive towards other humans and animals, thus early proper socialization will assist in thwarting this type of aggressive behavior. Expose them to your household's inhabitants, environment, routine and rules of conduct.

Begin gradually socializing your puppy from the day you bring him home. Proper early socialization that continues throughout your puppy's lifetime will provide you with a well-adjusted dog that is able to handle almost any situation in a calm manner and look to you, the alpha, for guidance.

Early, thorough, and continual socialization is important for your Mini Australian Shepherd. You do not want your dog acting territorial and wary of strangers, so it is important to expose them early to a variety of situations, animals, people and places. Socialization benefits you and your dog by providing you with a peace of mind and that you can expose your pup to different situations with the assurance that he will look to you for guidance in rules of etiquette for the indoor and outdoor world. Socialization is a foundation for all dogs throughout their lifetimes.

Before you begin your training sessions, it is a good idea to let your dog burn off some steam through exercise. He will be more focused and calm. Due to their intellect and willingness to obey, Mini Aussies are quick learners and love to perform. Be aware to use variety in training and treats. They do not respond well to repetitive training. It is common for a Mini Aussie to tear off running around the yard or house to burn excess energy.

Although intelligent, spunky and ready to work, sometimes Mini Aussies require more repetitions and training sessions before regularly obeying commands at a high percentage, but don't get frustrated. You will discover that they have individual personalities and that some will learn and retain commands quickly, while others will take more time and training sessions before responding at an extremely high rate, but once they learn a command they don't forget it. I recommend regular lifetime practice of all commands to keep them sharp.

Focus on the basics first and spend a lot of time on stay, come, no, leave it, and leash training. These commands obeyed at a high percentage will help you to keep your Mini Aussie out of harm's way. They are fast and eager to engage in chasing prey or to round up animals and children. They are also intelligent and if they put their mind to solving a problem can usually work out a solution. Their bigger versions are master escape artists and capable climbers; although the Mini versions are smaller never underestimate their fortitude to get their way.

The amount of herding ability that your Mini Aussie will display depends upon its recent breeding and individual personality. If you notice it early then spend extra time on shaping their behavior so that they understand nipping and bumping of humans is not allowed. If you require their herding abilities then begin teaching them in their youth to approach their animal charges calmly.

When training the come command outside, use a long check chord leash about 20 feet (six meters) or more, especially when you leave the yard and head to an open field or park. These leashes are also handy for fieldwork, sports and tracking.

Although very intelligent, don't be surprised if your Aussie decides not to obey every time you issue a command. This is where rewarding them with what they desire most helps you during training. It might be chasing a disc or a ball that is a huge pleasure to them, and thus a reward. Of course, it could be a simple "Atta girl" that allows them to feel special. You will figure it out and then use it to your advantage. Don't be afraid to keep their favorite pleasure from them when they are acting out in anyway or not obeying your commands. – This works.

Knowing what you want to train your Mini Aussie to do is as important as training your dog. You can begin training almost immediately, at around six weeks of age. A puppy is a blank slate and does not know any rules, therefore it is a wise idea to make a list and have an understanding of how you would like your puppy to behave.

What are the household rules and proper dog etiquette? As he grows, the same principle applies and you may adjust training from the basics to more specialized behaviors, such as making your dog a good travel, hiking, agility or simply a companion dog. Know what conditions and circumstances you plan to expose your dog or puppy to outside of the household and strategize to be prepared for those encounters by slowly introducing your dog to those situations.

Establish yourself as the pack leader from the time you first bring your new dog or puppy home. Being the alpha leader assists in the training process, and your dog's relationship with you and your family. Life is much easier for your dog if you are in charge, leading and providing for his needs.

Leading as the alpha assists in the act of working together with your dog towards the goal of understanding the rules of conduct and obedience. Your dog will be at ease when the rules are understood. Training should be an enjoyable bonding time between you and your dog.

Remember that there is no set time limit defining when your dog should learn, retain and then obey commands. Use short training sessions and be aware that if either of you are tired, it is recommended that you stop and try again later. If something does not seem quite right with your dog, in any way, have him checked out by a veterinarian. An unseen mental or physical illness could be impeding your dog's training progress.

An effective incentive is to make everything you do seem fun. This is done with cheerful voice, praise, and all around lighthearted demeanor. Always refrain from forcing your puppy to do anything they do not want to do. Highly prized treats are usually a great incentive to do something, and you will find that a fun, pleasant, friendly, happy, vocal tone combined with the treats will be ample reward for good behaviors and command compliance. Begin training all new commands indoors. This includes silencing all of your audio-visual devices that act as distractions to dog's sensitive ears and your attention.

If you notice any negative behavioral issues and are not quite sure if you are offering your dog proper socialization and necessary training, do not hesitate to enter your puppy into a puppy kindergarten class to assist you with training and socialization.

Behavioral issues do not have to be present to enroll your dog into a puppy kindergarten; this assistance will benefit the both of you. Properly research the available classes so that their approach matches your own. The time to enroll your puppy is usually around eight to ten weeks of age, and after their first round of shots, although some kindergarten classes will not accept puppies until they are three to four months of age.

Reward good behaviors, but do not reward for being cute, sweet, loveable, or huggable. If you wish to reward your dog, always reward after you issue a command and your dog obeys the command. During your training sessions, be sure to mix it up by adding a variety of toys and treats and never forgetting to have fun.

An easy way to avoid the onset of many different behavioral problems is to give your dog's ample daily exercise to keep them fit healthy and keep destructive behavioral problems at bay. Always provide consistent structure, firm but fair authority, rule enforcement, and importantly, love and affection. By maintaining and balancing these things, you will help to create a loyal companion and friend.

1. Timing is crucial when rewarding good behaviors and making corrections for bad behavior. Rewarding and correcting must be done right when the action occurs, otherwise the dog will be confused why it is being rewarded or corrected.

2. Patience and consistency are your allies in the training game.

3. Only train 1 command per session. Puppies only have the attention span to go about 5 - 10 minutes per session, and never exceed 15 minutes. Training a command once per day is enough for your dog to begin to learn and retain it. You can train different commands in different sessions.

It is easy to perform at least 3-5 training sessions in a day, but whenever the opportunity presents itself, you should reinforce the training sessions throughout the day.

For example, when opening a door or putting down a food bowl, first command him to sit, down or stay and be sure not to reward your dog unless he obeys. The most important thing to remember is to remain relaxed, keep it fun, and enjoy this time of bonding and training your puppy.

Five to 10 minutes per session is a good time limit for young puppies. Some remain puppies longer than others and may not fully develop until year 2; however, as dogs mature they will begin to focus for longer periods. Use a variety and an abundance of different treats and rewards.

4. All dogs have their own personalities and therefore respond to training differently. You need to account for individual personalities and adjust accordingly. If needed, do not hesitate to solicit professional help and advice, but by carefully observing your dog, you should be able to adjust your training.

5. We all love treats, and so does your dog. Giving your dog a treat is the best way to reinforce good behavior, to help change his behavior or just to make your dog perform that insanely funny dance-like thing. Remember, you do not want your pup filling up on treats as it might spoil dinner and interfere with his attention span, and large treats take time to chew and swallow, thus interrupting the session.

6. Keep a container of treats handy with you at all times. You do not want to miss a chance to reward a good behavior or reinforce a changed behavior. Always carry treats when you go on a walk.

Remember what treats your dog likes most and save those for special times, like the big breakthrough. In addition, what you consider a treat and what your dog considers a treat are 2 vastly different things. A single malt scotch or chicken wings might be a treat in your mind, but dried liver bits or beef jerky will be to your dog.

7. Ask for something before you give the treat. Tell your dog to sit, stay, or lie down, print 2 copies of your resume, anything, before you reward your dog with treats, petting or play. By asking for good behavior before you give your dog a reward, you demonstrate you are in charge in an easy and fun manner.

There is a common misconception that dogs are selfless and want to behave only to please, and out of respect for, you. This is horse pucky. This line of thinking is incorrect and detrimental to your success with the training. You have to make sure that your dog knows exactly why he should be listening to you, and exactly what action you want from him. You are the leader, the keeper of the treats, the provider of the scratching and the purveyor of toys. Keep this balance of power and the results will be your reward.

8. Be positive. Think about what you want your dog to do, instead of what you don't want him to do. Do not send mixed messages. Simply ignore the bad behaviors and reward your dog when he does the action you request. Begin with the basics, teach your dog some simple commands to communicate what you want, such as sit, come, stay, drop it and leave it.

9. There will be times before a training session that you will need to use a little exercise to release some of your dog's energy; this can increase his ability to focus during the session.

10. It is very important that you make sure your dog is comfortable in all sorts of situations. All dogs, even your sweet tempered pup, have the potential to bite. Making sure he is comfortable in various situations and teaching your dog to be gentle with his mouth will reduce the risk of

unwanted bites. Mouthing should not be acceptable behavior because it leads to potentially harmful actions.

11. Kids are great, are they not? However, the notion that kids and dogs are as natural a pairing as chocolate and peanut butter is simply not true. Kids are often bitten by dogs because they unintentionally do things that frighten dogs. Sometimes a child's behavior appears like prey to a dog.

Never leave a dog and a child together unsupervised, even if the dog is good with children. Teach children not to approach dogs that are unfamiliar to them. The way a child behaves with a familiar family dog may not be appropriate with another dog that they meet for the first time. Instruct children that tail pulling, hugging their necks tightly, leg pulling and hard head pats are unacceptable.

12. There exists many different ways to train puppies. Using clicker and reward-based training is an effective and humane way to train dogs and treat them with kindness.

Lying ahead of you will be the task of navigating your Mini Aussie's unique personality, which will affect your training and relationship. Although, you have no doubt read and watched much about training, spoken with friends and breeders, your dog's unique personality is why it is imperative to keep an open mind and use your intuition to guide you while training - be flexible.

13. Your consent as the owner is the one thing that will allow your dog to become disobedient, out of control and possibly a danger to your family and the outside world.

Therefore, arming yourself with knowledge about dog behaviors, and understanding your own dog's personality, will greatly assist you throughout the training process and being a companion to your dog. It is your responsibility to guide and train your dog to be a socially adjusted, obedient dog so that the two of you have a fruitful relationship. Well-behaved dogs are welcomed anywhere and your goal should be to train your dog to be well behaved and obedient.

Training Landmarks

A. Avoid future problems by correcting issues early and stopping bad behaviors before they escalate. This is accomplished through a lot of supervised time together.

B. Begin training on the first day that your puppy arrives home. Do not force anything, but as the trainer keep all of this in mind.

- Immediately begin establishing the household's rules.

- Begin housetraining.

- Begin chew-toy training.

- Begin minimal socialization.

C. Common achievement timelines should be set up for completion. Note these on your training calendar and keep track of your puppy's progress. These milestones and your training progress will let you know if you need to solicit help in any of the following.

1. Socialization to humans by 12 weeks.

2. Biting/nipping training successful by 18 weeks.

3. Well socialized by 5 months of age. At this stage your dog can meet and greet other humans and animals in a calm, friendly manner. Your dog handles transportation well and understands the basic etiquette for strange encounters. Meeting this goal will set the foundations for your adult dog to have good manners and be trustworthy. Keep in mind that socialization is a lifetime endeavor.

4. Housetraining completion ranges from 6 months to 12 months. Dog size and personality contribute to the training length of time. By 4 months most puppies often know to wait, but might still have issues. Many puppies are housetrained by 6 to 8 months, or mostly trained by 6 months with occasional accidents.

Examples of mentally stimulating activities for your Mini Aussie

- Retrieval games are physically and mentally stimulating.

- Agility games that are physical, but primarily mental, you can turn your household items into a course.

-Tracking, this uses dog's natural scenting abilities to find hidden objects.

- Herding trials or tests allow dogs to use their natural or trained herding abilities.

- Free play with other familiar dogs assists in socialization, energy release, and stimulation.

- Trick performance that is rewarded with access to your dog's highly valued items.

- Obedience classes.

- Flyball for physical activity.

- Hide and Seek with family members is good physical exercise for all.

- Working livestock is challenging both mentally and physically.

- Treibball is a relatively new dog sport where dogs gather and move large balls that represent a flock of animals.

Herding Breed Traits

I am including information on herding dogs to offer you the owner and trainer further insight into the characteristics these types of dog carry with them in their pedigree. The more information known about your Mini Aussie heritage, the better you will be equipped to train and understand him.

Herding dogs were originally bred for working or herding stock. They are referred to as working, stock, or herding dogs. The characteristics of this breed features heightened herding instincts derived from ancient hunting capabilities. Early in human history, dogs and humans began living and working with one another, relying on each other for survival. Humans began developing the herding breeds to manage domesticated animals, while simultaneously developing other breeds as guardians to protect the flocks from all types of predators. Herding and guarding dogs work together to keep the livestock together and safe.

For example, the Great Pyrenees Mountain Dogs steadfastly handle the guarding duties while the Pyrenean Shepherds diligently take care of the herding duties. Herders are known for their abilities to obey vocal and whistle commands, as well as think and act independently while performing their jobs.

Depending upon the different recognitions and classifications, I uncovered eighty-eight herding breeds in the world. The Herding Group is made up of sheep and cattle dogs that were, and are still bred to round up livestock and retrieve all stragglers.

Herding dogs use a variety of techniques, such as nipping, barking, running, and engaging in intense eye contact with their animal charges. Australian Kelpies and Aussies are known to run atop sheep (backing sheep) to move them along, and Border Collies are known for their staring and crouching style that enables them to mesmerize and herd almost any animal. Australian Cattle Dogs (Blue/Red Heelers) will nip at heels, or if necessary jump up to nip under a cows neck. The Mini Aussie's herding style is more upright than a Border Collie who crouches and stares down its herd. Mini Aussies also tend to move in towards the stock at a quicker rate than Border Collies.

Fearless, intelligent, alert, independent, and blessed with stamina and intense energy levels, these herding breeds possess the natural traits necessary to accomplish their jobs proficiently. Beyond their herding abilities, some in this group are used as police, guide and therapy dogs.

Versatility allows many of these breeds to herd cattle, ducks, geese, sheep, and goats, and the Mini Aussie is part of this group. Additionally, they will herd children, household pets, other dogs, and if not tethered they will even attempt to round up motor vehicles.

Because of their natural instincts, herding breeds that do not have a job and are to be household pets will need to be vigorously exercised and given opportunities to complete tasks. This can be accomplished through agility training, tracking games, herding trials, daily accompaniment with their humans on bike rides, jogs, hikes, runs, brisk walks or anything that will help deplete their seemingly endless energy reserves.

A herder that is not having their exercise needs met can become destructive, aggressive or display other negative behaviors. Before bringing home a herding dog, you must be certain that you can provide the proper amount of exercise and stimulation for these breeds. Most herding breeds need a few exercise outings per day, which should include a minimum of two hours of rigorous exercise.

Herding dogs come in a variety of coat types, heights, and weights. For example, the little Corgi's stand only 10 - 12 inches (25 - 30 cm) tall, while the French Beauceron stands 26–28 in (66–71 cm) tall. Most herders reside in the medium to large size classification. Amazingly, the little Corgi's are wonderfully efficient herding dogs that have been around since the Vikings brought them to Wales almost two thousand years ago. Since at least the 10th century, the little Pembroke Welsh Corgi has been herding cattle, ducks, geese, horses, and sheep. In recent times, herding dogs have been employed to keep ducks and geese clear of golf courses and airports.

Many in this group, including Mini Aussie, tend to be wary of strangers, but form tight loyal bonds with their handlers and family. They make a great addition as a family companion and enjoy being in the company of their humans. Nipping is something that needs to be addressed early when they are puppies. Always supervise your dog around small children. When children are running around playing, your herding dog immediately recognizes this as a herd to be tended, and they will begin nipping at the children's heels. You can sometimes observe them instinctually circling a group of children, in classic herding behavior. They do not intend to do harm, but a nip or hard bump can be painful and should not be allowed.

Early and ongoing socialization will help with aggression, possessiveness, territorialism and other potential negative behaviors that can surface. Herders are happiest when they have a purpose. These are some of the most intelligent and active dog breeds, and they have a strong predisposition for work.

The AKC created The Herding Group in 1983, and it is the newest American Kennel Club classification. Before the creation of their own group, these breeds were classified in the Working Group. In fact, this group has some of the most intelligent of all dog breeds. The Border Collie has been ranked as one of the most intelligent of all breeds. Other herding breeds ranked inside the top ten of some lists include the Australian Cattle Dog, German Shepherd, Shetland Sheepdog (Sheltie), and the Rottweiler.

10 Dog Communication

Training your Mini Aussie seems like a daunting task, but it is a unique and rewarding experience. It is the foundation of a healthy and long relationship with your new dog or puppy. You must be the one in charge of the relationship and lead with a pack leader mentality, showing patience and love. Whether you choose to enroll your dog in an obedience school such as the Sirius® reward training system or go it alone at home, you will the need assistance of quality books like this one, videos, and articles to help guide you through the process and offer solutions to obstacles along the way.

Without a doubt, it is nice to have an obedient friend by your side through good and bad times. Owning a dog is a relationship that needs tending throughout the years. Once you begin training, it will continue throughout the life of your dog friend.

An obedient dog is easier to care for and causes less household problems and expense. You know what needs to be done, but what about your dog? How do you read his messages regarding what you are attempting to accomplish? I am going to cover dogs' body language and vocal language to provide an insight into what your dog is attempting to communicate. This should prove to be an asset while training your dog.

The art of dogmanship has been described as a partnership of species in which instinct and intuition are utilized over logical thought to enable work in collaboration. Humans need to be flexible and responsive, and able not only to lead, but also to follow. Humans need to open their sensory awareness and place high importance upon non-verbal communications.

It is further defined as the understanding of how dogs communicate with one another in their own canine language and being able to communicate with dogs in their language. When you understand some or most of the techniques dogs use to communicate with each other, you can then apply them when communicating with dogs yourself.

To do this you have to be able to isolate your human emotions and put the needs of the dog at the forefront. When a dog is born into this world, environmental and genetic factors will affect that dog's behavior. Additionally they have behaviors coded into their DNA that dictates their inherent canine behaviors. In dog-to-dog communication, every gesture and vocalized sound has meaning. These can be exceptionally subtle and difficult for humans to see and interpret.

Although dogs are intelligent and can learn human communication methods, it is not always the most efficient way to communicate with a dog. Dogs are simpler than humans and it is more challenging to teach a dog to understand human communication than it is to use dog communication methods to communicate with your dog.

If a person is able to be open up to the idea, then they can learn the language dogs use to communicate with each other and incorporate that into their communication with dogs. Using this method, you begin to work in harmony with your dog and his natural instincts, instead of against them.

Commonly humans forget to address or never consider what a dog's natural instincts are. Embedded in their genetic code is the thirst for rules, boundaries and structure. Dogs enjoy knowing what the rules of etiquette for all situations are, and having the structure of a daily schedule for walks, playtime, exercise and feedings. They also crave consistency in actions, and this is something that some humans regularly struggle to provide.

Therefore, it is essential to provide your dog with the things that they need, such as physical and mental exercises, leadership, play, toys, rule establishment and enforcement, and the essentials that are food, water, shelter, love, kindness and all the other things that dogs need to live a fruitful life.

The entire family should understand the rules of etiquette for your dog so that rule enforcement is always the same. An example of failed consistency is if your daughter is reprimanding your dog for an action that you allow. This creates conflict in your dog's brain. Your dog will not know which way to act and this will cause your dog distress and possibly anxiety that can lead to further dysfunctional idiosyncrasies.

Human behavior can have an entirely different meaning to a dog, and this is why commonly a dog owner may be perplexed by his dog's behavior. The owner is thinking in human terms and not in dog terms. Negative dog behaviors are mostly because something is missing from their life, and instead of blaming a dog for its behavior, we must figure out the root cause of the negative behavior and remedy it, thus showing our leadership abilities and doing our job as their leader.

A dog's temperament is shaped by the owner's ability to provide him with what he instinctually needs. Educating yourself about dog communication and behaviors is your first step to understanding natural canine communications (dogmanship). Owning and properly caring for a dog requires a knowledge base that has been diagramed and written about to help you learn through personal observation. Studying your dog's behaviors and allowing your intuition to guide you will enable you to learn dog communication techniques

Using Human Body Language to Communicate

There are a couple of important things to keep in the forefront of your mind regarding human movements around all dogs. The first is a tough one to master. *Stay calm even when you are not. Avoid fast, erratic movements such as jumping back, making a loud noise when surprised or frightened, and flinging your arms into the air. These types of movement mimic prey or the dog can mistake these movements for a type of game that they want to play.

The dog's reaction might be that it attempts to put its mouth around your fast moving limbs, jumps up or give chase to you. The difficult part when you are surprised or nervous is to freeze in place and avoid eye contact while simultaneously slightly turning your head away. If you feel it is necessary, fold your arms to your chest. If you need to move away from a dog, then use slow fluid movements while backing away from the dog.

Startled people sometimes hold their breath, so do not forget to breathe and stay calm. A dog may perceive your held breath as a sign that you are tense and going to react. This could escalate tensions.

Eye contact is very important to dogs and assists you in conveying to your dog that you are serious and in command. Always use direct eye contact when issuing commands or calling your dog by name.

If a dog jumps up on to you the best method is not to engage with your eyes, fold your arms across your chest and freeze in place. In essence, you are to avoid to the best of your ability any physical or eye engagement with the dog.

Jumping dogs usually want attention but when they continually do not get that attention, they begin to catch onto the fact that jumping is an unwanted and undesirable behavior.

I realize that their claws might hurt you, and some dogs are large enough to move you, so do the best that you can to ignore the dog and not make any sudden movements. This is covered further in the training chapter on jumping.

Dogs can sense our inner feelings by the way we use our tone of voice, body language and facial expressions. They are able to read people much better than most people can read a dog's body language. Their keen abilities to observe us intensely are used by them to interpret and anticipate what we want from them. Using the correct body language helps you when meeting unfamiliar dogs, and in controlling your own dog.

The following is an example of how a dog interprets human actions. If you approach a submissive dog by leaning forward towards him and then move your hand towards his head, it will usually result in a negative reaction because you are acting out a dominant behavior and he is therefore intimidated by you. Since the dog has already taken the submissive posture, the dog is not expecting a dominant action.

Conversely, if you approach the same dog by first crouching down beside him and then bringing your hand from his chest up to his head, this should produce a different reaction. Our instinct is to pet dogs on their head, but when interacting with a submissive dog it is better to pet their chest to avoid intimidation and then if it is going well, slowly move to their head.

"How do I identify a submissive dog?" That is a good question and the answer will help you in many ways. A submissive dog will commonly lower its head and tail making its body smaller, while simultaneously avoiding eye contact. Sometimes owners mistake this for a dog feeling sad, when in fact, it is submitting to the owner and showing by their body posture that the owner is the leader.

If your dog is showing this submissive posture, this means that you have achieved the alpha position and your dog is following your lead. Your dog is happy because he is comforted in knowing that he has a leader that is taking good care of him. A happy and secure submissive dog that lowers itself is not a dog that is recklessly jumping around vying for attention and trying to control its owner.

Realizing what the submissive posture is and not falsely thinking that your dog is upset or sad will help you not to send your dog confusing signals. The fact that your dog is showing this posture instead of jumping on you and trying to steer you is a good sign and does not mean that you need to cheer your dog up or act differently to address the posture.

A submissive posture is not to be mistaken for fear, cowering or avoidance-type actions. Dogs in this posture that display unwarranted fear when a person reaches to touch them, or while being touched or engaged, have often been abused or simply are not used to strangers or affection (handling) the way well-treated and trained dogs are. Abused dogs often skulk at a distance and avoid eye contact while making their bodies small in an attempt to remain unnoticed. This is far different from a healthy, submissive posture.

Body Language in Training

Have you ever had trouble with your dog obeying your come command? Try this body movement. Instead of becoming angry, yelling, or begging, turn your back and crouch down. This position tells your dog that he is not in trouble and that you are not a threat to him. Do not repeatedly say the come command. This body position is an invitation instead of a demand. Often this position works, and when your dog comes to join you, always reward him.

As a last resort, you can try running away from your dog. This will commonly be perceived as play and often your dog will come running. If your dog is not obeying, continue to work on training your dog to obey the all-important come command so that you do not have to resort to these physical cues.

Maybe you have not been offering a good enough reason for your dog to come and need to improve your rewards, he has not retained the command, or you are still earning the dog's respect. Whatever the case, practice until your dog comes to you at your command at least 90% of the time. The come command is extremely important for the safety of your dog and your peace of mind.

In leash training, body language plays an important role. Every time your dog is pulling, you should change direction and walk the other way. Using this body language, you are teaching him that you are the one in control and decide the direction and speed that you walk.

In addition, when you are walking your dog on a leash, you want him to maintain a close distance but never impede your walking and direction changes. If your dog is not keeping the proper distance and not moving with you, but instead crowding you, slightly bumping him while changing direction will stop him from crowding or impeding you while you walk. This can be practiced during training sessions that include many direction changes and serpentine walking. Your dog must know that you are in charge and you make the rules. Soon he will learn not to crowd or impede you so that the two of you can harmoniously walk with a loose leash.

Body language is equally important to communicating with dogs as it is with humans, but the difference is that communicating with humans comes naturally to us. Standing upright, remaining calm, confident, and consistent is how all alphas should act when directing their dogs, and if you notice, many powerful people do the same when interacting with other people. Keep this in the forefront of your mind, and the more you practice, the more natural and easy it will become.

It takes practice to be able to control our reactions, facial expressions and tones. Having this type of control helps some people to be better trainers than others. Remember that you are under constant observation from your dog and they respect a confident leader. Whenever you act less confident, your dog will immediately notice it.

Enjoying the dog training process and having a good time with your dog is also important, so do not be afraid to laugh and smile. You don't have to be unemotional or act like a statue while learning about dogs and yourself.

Learning Natural Dog Behaviors

Remember that we cannot always read a dog's body language accurately. All dogs have their own unique personality, therefore they will express themselves in individual ways. It is possible that a dog's happy wagging tail could be another dog's way of conveying that it is nervous or anxious. A dog's breed, size, or appearance are not proper indicators of whether a dog will bite, but his body language is. Keep it in your thoughts when reading a dog's body language that it is difficult to be 100% accurate when interpreting it and to use caution around strange dogs.

In my books, I cover some frequent dog positions and body language, but I realized more visual clues are needed. I found 2 handy free downloads at the ASPCA and American Humane websites with photographs of dog postures. The diagrams and descriptions will assist you to identify what a dog's body language and postures are usually stating.

Use the information to observe your dog and verify if he is consistently using a body posture or movement that illustrates his mood and whether it corresponds with the diagrams. It is a good idea to keep a journal and log your observations so that you know what your dog is saying to you with his body movements.

When practicing reading dog body language, you will note that some dogs have curly spitz-type tails and therefore it will take a keen eye to see and denote what their tail position might be conveying so you will have to rely more on facial, ear, mouth and body postures. It is more difficult to read breeds with docked tails, flat faces or which are black in color. From a distance black-colored dogs' facial expressions can be difficult to see. Creating further difficulties are breeds that have puffy hair, long hair, or extensive hair that hides their physical features.

Observing your dog's ears, eyes, lips, mouth, body postures and tail movements, and then matching them to your dog's emotional state, will take some time, but when you begin to easily identify and understand your dog's emotions and intentions from his body language, you are well on your way to a better, long-lasting relationship. Additionally, you will improve your training and communication skills with your dog and other people's dogs. This is your first step to mastering dogmanship. This skill can only be learned through the observation of dogs, trusting in your intuition, and in tandem with studying about dog communication.

Using daily focused observations, you will gradually become aware of your dog's communications and their meanings. Some dogs' body language is easy to see and define so do not feel overwhelmed or intimidated by the process that I have outlined. Previous dog owners will attest that the more time spent with dogs the more you glean from their behaviors. Gradually you will become more aware of dog behavior and then subtle changes will occur in the way that you interact with dogs. The process is enjoyable because you are spending time with your dog companion. All dog trainers are continuously honing their dog language skills.

Body Language

What is body language? Body language is all of the non-verbal communication we exhibit when engaged in an exchange with another entity. Every one of those little tics, spasms, and movements that we act out comprise non-verbal body language. Studies state that over 50% of how people judge us is based on our use of body language. Apparently, the visual interpretation of our message is equal to our verbal message.

It is interesting that some studies indicate that when body language disagrees with the verbal message, our verbal message accounts for as little as 7-10% of how others judge us. With that kind of statistic, I would say that body language is extremely important for communication.

Similar to humans, dogs use their bodies to communicate. Their audio and visual senses are especially acute. Observe how your dog tilts his head, moves his limbs and what actions his tail is making. They are continuously reading us in the same manner.

The Tail

A wagging tail does not mean that a dog is friendly. With most dogs that have tails it can convey many messages, some nice, some nasty. Specialists say a dog's wagging tail can mean the dog is scared, confused, preparing to fight, confident, concentrating, interested, or happy.

"How do you tell the difference?"

Look at the speed and range of motion in the tail. The wide and fast tail wag is usually the message of "Hey, I am so happy to see you!" wag. The tail that is not tight between the hind legs, but instead is sticking straight back horizontally means the dog is curious but unsure, and probably not going to bite but remain in a place of neutral regard. This dog will probably not be confrontational, yet the verdict is not in. The slow tail wag means the same; the dog's friendly meter is gauging the other as friend or foe.

The tail held high and stiff, or bristling (hair raised) is a WATCH OUT! -red flag warning humans to be cautious. This dog may not only be aggressive, but dangerous and ready to rumble. If you come across this dog, it is time to calculate your retreat and escape plan.

Not only should the speed and range of the wag be recognized while you are reading doggie body language, one must also take note of the tail position. A dog that is carrying its tail erect is a self-assured dog in control of itself. On the flip side of that, the dog with their tail between their legs, tucked in tight is the "I surrender man, I surrender, please don't hurt me" posture.

The chill dog, a la reggae special, is the dog that has her tail lowered but not tucked in between her legs. The tail that is down and relaxed in a neutral position states the dog is relaxed.

While training your dog or simply playing, it is a good idea to take note of what his or her tail is doing and determine if your dog's tail posture is matching their moods. Your understanding of your dog's tail movements and body posture will be of great assistance throughout its lifetime.

Up Front

On the front end of the dog are the head and ears that have their special motions. A dog that cocks her head or twitches her ears is giving the signal of interest and awareness, but sometimes it can indicate fear. The forward or ear up movements can show a dog's awareness of seeing or hearing something new. Due to the amazingly acute canine sense of hearing, this can occur long before we are aware of anything. These senses are two of the assets that make dogs so special and make them fantastic guard and watchdogs.

"I give in, and will take my punishment", is conveyed by having the head down and ears back. Take note of this submissive posture, observe the neck, and back fur for bristling. Sometimes this accompanies this posture. Even though a dog is giving off this submissive stance, if it is showing bristling it should be approached with caution because it may feel threatened and launch an attack thinking it needs to defend himself.

"Smile, you are on camera." Yep, you got it, dogs smile too. It is usually a subtle corner pull back to show the teeth. Do not confuse this with the obvious snarl that entails a raised upper lip and bared teeth, sometimes accompanied by a deep growling sound. The snarl is something to be extremely cautious of when encountered. A snarling dog is not joking around - the snarl is serious. This dog is ready to be physically aggressive.

The Whole Kit and Caboodle

Using the entire body, a dog that rolls over onto its back and exposes his belly, neck and genitals is conveying the message that you are in charge. A dog that is overly submissive sometimes urinates a small amount to express his obedience towards a human or another dog.

Front paws down, rear end up, tail is a waggin'. This, "Hut, hut, hut, c'mon Sparky hike the ball," posture is the ole K-9 position of choice for, "Hey! It is playtime, and I am ready to go!" This posture is sometimes accompanied with a playful bark and/or pawing of the ground in an attempt to draw you into his playful state. I love it when a dog is in this mood, although they can be aloof to commands when in such a mood.

Whines, Growls, Howls, Barks and Yelps. Sounds Dogs Make

We just had a look at the silent communication of body language. Now, I will look into the doggie noises we cherish, but sometimes find annoying.

"Just what is our dog trying to tell us?" Our canine friends often use vocal expressions to get their needs met. Whines and growls mean what they say, so when training your dog, listen carefully. As you become accustomed to the dog's vocal communication, and are able to begin understanding them, the happier you will both become. Some canine noises can be annoying and keep you awake, or wake you up. These may require your attention and be trained as inappropriate vocalizations.

Barking

"What does a dog bark say and why bark at all?" Dogs bark to say, "Hey, what's up dude?" "I am hungry," "Look at me!" or "Want to play?" A bark may warn of potential trouble, or to convey that the dog is bored or lonely. I think we all know that stimulated and excited dogs also bark.

It is up to us to survey the surroundings and assess the reason. We need to educate ourselves about our dog's various barks so we can act appropriately. Not every bark is a put on your slippers, grab a flashlight and patrol the house late at night bark.

Whining and Whimpering

Almost from the time they are freshly made and feeding upon their mother's milk, our little puppies begin to make their first little furball noises. Whimpering or whining to get their mother's attention to feed or for comfort is innate and, as a result, they know mom will come to them. They also use these two W's on us to gain our attention.

Other reasons for whimpering or whining are from fear produced by loud noises such as thunderstorms or fireworks. I think most of us have experienced the 4th of July phenomenon where the entire dog population is barking excessively until the wee hours of the morning when the last fireworks are ignited, and the final "BOOM!" dies off. Whining can also come from separation anxiety, but if your dog is whining for attention, you should not indulge him.

Growling

Growling means that you had better be acutely aware of the dog's intentions and what it is doing. Usually a dog that is growling is seriously irritated and preparing to be aggressive. However, this is not always true, sometimes a dog will issue a growl to request that they are petted more. It is our job to learn the difference with our pooches.

Howling

Picture the dark silhouette of a howling dog with a full moon backdrop. A dog's howl is a distinct vocalization that most dogs use, and every wolf makes. Howling can mean loneliness, desire, warning or excitement. A lonely howl is a dog looking for a response. Dogs also howl after a long hunt when they have tracked and cornered their prey. Some scent hounds use a distinct sound called a 'bay'.

CANINE BODY LANGUAGE

CALM & NEUTRAL

RELAXED

ALERT

ANXIOUS & NERVOUS

PLAYFUL

DOMINANT

FRIGHTENED

EXCITED

AGGRESSIVE

SUBMISSIVE

11 Housetraining Your Mini Aussie

When you first bring your peeing and pooping machine home, clip on his leash and carry him to the predetermined waste elimination spot that you and your family have chosen. Let your pup eliminate then take him inside the home. Now that you have established his elimination spot, remind the family that that is where your pup should be taken each time he has to eliminate.

It is a fact that dogs are a bit particular about where they "relieve" themselves and will invariably build a strong habit. While housetraining your Mini Aussie, remember that whenever he soils somewhere in the house, a strong preference is being built towards that particular area. This is why preventing soiling accidents is very important; additionally thoroughly cleaning the area where the defecation or urination has occurred is tremendously important. When your puppy does relieve himself in the house, blame yourself not your pup.

Until your puppy has learned where to do his business, you should keep a constant, watchful eye on him, whether he is in his crate, on a mat, beside you or in his pen. During housetraining, some people will tether their puppies to their waist or to a nearby object. This allows them to keep their puppy in their sight at all times and is a very good idea.

- When your pup is indoors but out of the crate, watch for sniffing or circling, and as soon as you see this behavior immediately take him outdoors. Do not hesitate.

- If your pup is having accidents in the crate, the crate may be too big. The crate should be big enough for your puppy to stand up, turn around, and lie down in. If crate accidents occur, remove any soiled items from the crate and thoroughly clean it.

- Keep your puppy confined to their specific gated puppy area where accidents can be easily cleaned, such as his pen or section of bathroom, pantry, laundry or similar room. Do not leave your puppy confined to their crate for hours upon end. You want their crate to be an enjoyable place that they find safe and comforting.

- Set a timer to go off every 45 minutes to an hour so that you remember to take your puppy out before nature calls. With progress, you can increase the time duration between elimination outings.

- A good rule of thumb for elimination outing frequencies is as follows:

- Up to 6 weeks of age, elimination should happen every 45 minutes to an hour.

- Two months of age, around every 2 to 3 hours.

- Three months, every 4 hours.

- Four months and up - around every 5 hours.

These times will vary with individual dogs.

- If your pup doesn't do his duty when taken outdoors, wait a few minutes and then bring your pup back indoors and keep a close eye on him. One option is to keep your pup tethered to your waist so that he is always in view, and then try again in 10-15 minutes.

- While you are away, if possible, arrange to have a person to take your puppy outside to eliminate because this will greatly speed up the housetraining process.

Establish a Schedule

- You should take your puppy out many times during the day, most importantly after eating, playing and sleeping.

Feed your puppy appropriate amounts of food 3 times per day and leave the food down for around 15 minutes at a time and then remove it. You can keep a pup's water down until about 8 at night, but then remove it from your puppy's reach. This will help with accidents and reduce you having to wake up in the night to endure the elements while he does his business.

- When you hear him whining, take him out for elimination once during the night. Puppies can usually hold their bladders for about 4-5 hours during sleep. Dogs do not like to soil their own area and only as a last resort will they soil their crate or bedding.

- Gradually, your puppy will be able to hold his urine for increasingly longer lengths of time, but until then keep to the hourly schedule unless he is sleeping, but always take him out after waking. Having your puppy's excrement and urine outdoors puts your puppy's housetraining on the fast track.

Consistency Is the Mother of Prevention

Until your puppy is reliably housetrained, take him outside to the same spot each time and always leave a little bit of his waste there as a scent marker. This will be the designated relief spot and if you like can place a warning sign at that spot. Remember to use this spot for relief only and not for play. Bring your puppy to his spot and when you see him getting ready to eliminate waste, say something like, "Potty time," "Hurry up," or "Now."

As your pup is eliminating, do not speak because it will distract him and potentially interrupt full elimination. Instead, ponder how much fun it will be when he is playing fetch and running back to you. When your puppy finishes, praise, pet, give a top-notch treat and spend about five minutes playing with him.

If your puppy eliminates in the house, remember - that it is your fault. Maybe you went too quickly. If you see your puppy relieving himself indoors, quickly take him outside to the designated elimination spot so that he can finish there and, when he is done, offer praise for finishing in the correct spot.

Each time you find a mess, clean it thoroughly without your puppy watching you do it. Use a cleaner made specifically for pet stains so that there is no smell or evidence that you have failed him. This way it will not become a regular spot for your puppy and a new regular clean up chore for you. Regular outings should keep this chore to a minimum.

This Question Rings a Bell

"Can I teach my puppy when to tell me when he needs to go out?"

- Yes, you can! Hang a bell at dog level beside the door that is used to let your pup outdoors. Put a dab of easy cheese or peanut butter on the bell. When he touches the bell and it rings, immediately open the door. Repeat this every time and take him to the elimination spot. Eventually, he will ring the bell without the food on it and this will tell you when he needs to go outside.

Be careful here, your puppy may start to ring the bell when he wants to go outside to play, explore or for other non-elimination reasons. To avoid this, each time he rings the bell, only take him out to the elimination spot. If he starts to play, immediately bring him in the house reinforcing that the bell means elimination only.

Now that the schedule has been established and you know what you are supposed to do, keep in mind that puppies can generally hold their bladders for a good 1-hour stretch. Larger breeds of adult dogs can hold their bladders longer than smaller dog breeds and some small dogs cannot last the night before needing to go outside. Most adult dogs generally do not last longer than 8-10 hours between needing to urinate.

Housetriainng Timetable

1. Housetraining completion ranges from 6 months to 12 months.
2. A dog's personality contributes to the training length of time.
3. By 4 months most puppies often know to wait, but might still have issues.
4. Many puppies are housetrained by 6 to 8 months, or mostly trained by 6 months with occasional accidents lasting a further few months.

All dog owners are much happier after this training is completed but keep in mind that scolding your dog for doing a natural thing is not going to help you when housetraining. Rewarding him for the outdoor eliminations and avoiding indoor accidents is your gateway to success.

Of course, when you see your pup about to pee or poop indoors, a quick "No" as you sweep him up to take him outside might temporarily cease the activity so that you can whisk them outside before any waste hits the ground or possibly your hand or arm. Then as previously mentioned, praise him at the beginning of the outdoor elimination then remain quiet.

It isn't as difficult as it might read. Being active in housetraining will definitely speed up the process, but it does take a few months for puppies to increase their bladder abilities and to learn the rules.

Far too often new puppy owners are not around enough to follow the protocol efficiently and this regularly leads to housetraining taking longer. Some dogs learn suprisingly fast that outdoors is the only acceptable place to eliminate waste, but their bodies haven't matured to catch up to their brains, so please practice patience and understanding.

I am certain you will do a great job.

12 Teaching Your Dog the Joy of Handling

"Scratch a dog and you'll find a permanent job." ~ Franklin P Jones

Teaching your Mini Aussie to be still, calm and patient while being handled is a very important step in your relationship. When you master this one, it makes life easier for both of you when at home, the groomer or vet. Handling also helps when there is unwanted or accidental touching and especially when dealing with small children who love to handle dogs in all sorts of unusual ways. This one will take patience and a few tricks to get started. Remember that it is important to begin handling your new puppy immediately after you find each other and are living together.

The sooner your puppy accepts your touch and manipulations the easier life will be for the both of you because handling is needed for grooming, bathing, lifting, affection, medical procedures, inspecting for ticks, fleas and caring for injuries.

Recognize that muzzles are not bad and do not hurt dogs. They can be an effective device and a great safety feature when your dog is learning to be handled. Easy cheese or peanut butter spread on the floor or on the refrigerator door can keep your puppy in place while he learns to be handled. If your puppy does not like to be handled, he will slowly learn to accept it.

You must practice this with your puppy for at least 1 to 3 minutes each day so that he becomes comfortable with being touched everywhere. All Mini Aussies are unique and therefore some will accept this easier and quicker than others will. Handling training will be a life-long process but it is an enjoyable procedure.

With all of the following exercises, follow these 5 steps

1. Begin with short, non-intrusive, gentle touching. If your puppy is calm and not trying to squirm away, use a word such as "good", "nice", or "yes", and give your pup a treat.

73

2. If your puppy squirms, keep touching him but do not fight his movements, keeping your hand lightly on him while moving it with his squirms. Use your hand as though it were a suction cup and stuck to the place that you are touching. When he settles, treat him and remove your hand.

3. Work from 1 second to 10 seconds or more, gradually working your way up to touching for longer durations, such as 2, 4, 6, 8 to 10 seconds.

4. Do not go forward to another step until your puppy adapts, and enjoys the current step.

5. Do not work these exercises more than a couple of minutes at a time. Overstimulation can cause your puppy stress. Continue slowly at your puppy's preferred pace.

Handling the Body

Paws

It is a fact that most puppies do not like to have their paws touched. Proceed slowly with this exercise. The eventual goal is for your puppy to adore his paws being fondled.

In the following exercises, any time your puppy does not squirm and try to get away, click and treat your pup. If he does squirm, stay with him using gentle contact, and when your pup ceases wiggling, click and treat him, and then release him when he calms down. Each one of these steps will take a few days to complete and will require at least a dozen repetitions. *If you are not using the clicker, simply treat at the appropriate time.

Confirm that you have successfully completed each step and that your puppy is at least tolerant of the contact before moving on to the next one. Continue to regularly practice.

- Do each step with all 4 paws, and remember to pause a minute between paws, allowing your pup to regain his composure.

- Pick up your puppy's paw and immediately click and treat him. Repeat this 5 times and then continue by adding an additional 1 second each time you pick up his paw until 10 seconds is reached.

Hold the paw for 10 to 12 seconds ensuring your dog doesn't struggle. Begin with 2 seconds and then in different sessions work your way up to 12.

During holding the paw, begin adding the following:

- Hold the paw and move it around.

- Massage the paw.

- Pretend to trim the nails.

Side Note: Do not trim your dog's nails unless you are positively sure you know what you are doing. It is not easy and, if you are not properly trained, you can cause extreme pain to your dog.

The Collar

Find a quiet, low distraction place to practice, grab treats, and put your puppy's collar on him.

1. While gently restrained, touch your dog's collar underneath his chin, and then release it right away while simultaneously clicking and treating him. Do this about 10 times or until your puppy seems comfortable and relaxed with the process.

2. Grab and hold the collar where it is under his chin and hold it for about 2 seconds, C/T, and repeat. Increase the amount of time until you have achieved about 10 seconds of holding and your puppy remains calm. Click and treat after each elapsed amount of time. By increasing the hold time by 2 seconds each time, gradually work your way up to 10 seconds of holding. This may take several days and sessions.

3. Hold the collar under his chin and now give it a little tug. If he accepts this and does not resist, click and treat, and repeat. If he squirms, keep a gentle hold on the collar until he calms down, and then C/T and release him. Repeat this step until he is content with the procedure.

4. Now, switch to the top of the collar and repeat the whole progression again. Remember to slowly increase the time held and the intensity of the tug.

You can pull or tug, but do not jerk your puppy's neck or head because this can cause injury and interfere with the objectives of the training exercise. You can practice touching the collar while you are treating during training him other tricks. Gently hold the bottom or top of the collar when you are giving your dog a reward for successfully completing a commanded behavior.

Mouth

1. Gently touch your puppy's mouth, click and treat, and repeat 10 times.

2. Touch the side of your puppy's mouth and lift a lip to expose a tooth, click and treat, then release only after he stops resisting.

3. Gently and slowly, lift the lip to expose more and more teeth on both sides of the mouth, and then open the mouth. Then release when he does not resist, and click and treat. Be cautious with this one.

4. Touch a tooth with a toothbrush, then work up to brushing your puppy's teeth for 1 to 10 seconds, and then later increase the time. Brushing your puppy's teeth is something you will be doing a few times weekly for the lifetime of your dog.

Ears

1. Reach around the side of your puppy's head and then briefly and gently touch his ear. Click and treat, repeat 10 times.

2. When your puppy is comfortable with this, continue and practice holding the ear for 1 second. If he is calm, click and treat. If he squirms, stay with him until he is calm. When your puppy calms down, click and treat, and then release the ear. Do this until you can complete 10 seconds with no wiggling.

3. Maneuver your pup's ear and pretend that you are cleaning it. Do this gently and slowly so that your puppy learns to enjoy it. It will take a few days of practice until your puppy is calm enough to endure real ear cleaning. If your puppy is already sensitive about his ears being touched, it will take longer. See ear cleaning in the Basic Care section.

Proceed slowly at your puppy's comfortable pace. There is no rush, just the end goal of your pup enjoying being handled in all sorts of ways that are beneficial to him.

Tail

Many puppies are sensitive about having their tails handled, and rightly so. Think about if someone grabbed you by the arm and you were not fully ready. That is similar to how a puppy feels when grabbed, especially when their tails are handled.

1. Start by briefly touching the tail. When moving to touch your puppy's tail move slowly and let your hand be seen moving towards his tail. This keeps him from being startled. Repeat this 10 times with clicking and treating, until you notice your puppy is comfortable with his tail being touched.

2. Increase the length of time you hold his tail until you achieve the 10-second mark.

3. Tenderly and cautiously pull the tail up, brush the tail and then tenderly pull on it until your dog allows you to do this without reacting by jerking, wiggling or whimpering.

Your dog needs to be comfortable being touched on paws, ears, tail, mouth, and the rest of his body, and this should be practiced daily.

Brushing

- Get your puppy's brush and lightly touch him with it all over his body. If he remains unmoving, give him a click and treat and then repeat. Repeat this until you can brush every part of his body without him moving.

Children

You must prepare your poor pup to deal with the strange and unwelcome touching that is often exacted on them by children. Alternatively, you could just put a sign around his neck that says, "You must be at least 16 to touch this puppy". However, it is very likely that your puppy will encounter children that are touchy, grabby or pokey.

- Prepare your puppy for the strange touches that children may perpetrate by practicing while clicking and treating him for accepting these odd bits of contact, such as ear tugs, tail tugs, and perhaps a little harder than usual head pats, kisses and hugs. Keep in mind, as previously mentioned, puppies and kids are not a natural pairing, but cheese and wine are. Even a puppy that is good with kids can be pushed to his breaking point and then things can get ugly, and nobody wants that.

Always supervise children around your dog. ALWAYS! – It is a dog ownership law.

Your puppy will become comfortable with all varieties of touching and handling if you work slowly, patiently and with plenty of good treats. Handling training is a very important step in your dog's socialization.

13 Crate Training

Dogs need their own safe place to call home and relax. An owner's house might be a place to roam but it's not the den dogs crave. The crate satisfies a dog's longing for a den, and along with its many other uses provides comfort to them. All puppies should be taught to enjoy residing in their crate and know that it is a safe haven for them; therefore, it is important never to use it for punishment.

Before you begin crate training give your dog a couple of days to adjust to his new home and surroundings. A dog can undergo crate training at any age. A dog's love for their crate is healthy and assists you in taking care of him or her throughout their lifetime.

Try to limit your puppy's time in the crate to around 1 hour per session. Never leave your adult dog in a crate for longer than 5 hours without providing them time outside of the crate. As your puppy matures and has learned proper dog etiquette (not chewing everything in sight), is housetrained, and can be trusted to run freely around your house, you can then leave the door open so that they can use it for their private bungalow to come and go as they choose.

I have listed below the benefits of the crate, the things to avoid, the types, furnishing, the steps to crate train your dog, and troubleshooting - Godspeed.

Benefits of the Crate

1. It aids in housetraining because dogs are reluctant to soil their own sleeping area.

2. Acts as a mobile doghouse for trips via car, airplane, train and then to be used at destinations such as motels and foreign houses.

3. The mobility can be utilized inside your own home by being moved throughout the house. *Especially beneficial during housetraining when you want your puppy near you.

4. Can reduce separation anxiety.

5. Keeps your dog out of harm's way.

6. Assists him to develop a chew-toy addiction.

7. Aids your puppy in calming and quieting down.

Until he or she has learned that the chewing, tearing, and ripping of household and human items is forbidden, the crate will keep your dog separated from those items.

Things to Avoid

1. Do not use the crate as punishment. If used in this manner it will defeat the purpose and cause your dog to fear the crate instead of love it.

2. Avoid lengthy crating sessions. Long periods in the crate defer socialization, exercise, and can cause doggy depression, restlessness and anxiety.

3. Puppies have an issue holding their need to eliminate waste. Young puppies tend to go hourly, but as they mature, the time between eliminations lengthens. Keep this in mind for puppies and adult dogs, and always schedule elimination breaks. Set a timer to remind you to free your pooch from the crate to go outdoors.

A good rule of thumb for elimination intervals is as follows: up to 6 weeks of age - elimination every hour; at 2 months of age - around 2 to 3 hours; at 3 months - 4 hours; 4 months and up - around 5 hours. These times will vary with individual dogs.

If you are housetraining an adult dog, he or she might be able to hold their bowels longer, but have not yet learned that they are required to wait and go outdoors.

4. Soiled items. Quickly remove and clean any soiled items inside the crate, and thoroughly clean the crate with a non-toxic cleaner that will erase any signs of elimination.

5. Avoid crating your dog when your dog has not recently eliminated waste.

6. Avoid continued involuntary crating after your puppy is housetrained and he or she understands that damaging human property is forbidden; instead only use the crate when necessary. At this point they will come and go freely into and out of their crate, finding it a safe place to nap.

Buying, Furnishing, and Preparing the Crate

The time has come for you to go crate shopping and you notice that they come in many sizes and designs. Let the shopper in you compare the advantages and disadvantages of the different styles to figure out which will be best suited for your usage and dog. A few types are as follows: collapsible metal, metal with fabric, wire, solid plastic, fixed and folding aluminum, and soft-sided collapsible crates that conveniently fold up easily for travel.

Regarding traveling always have your dog safely secured when in a motor vehicle. There are crates specially designed and tested for vehicle transportation.

"What size crate do I purchase?"

The crate should be big enough for your puppy to stand up, turn around, and lie down in. If you wish to hedge your bet, instead of purchasing multiple crates you can purchase a crate that will accommodate your puppy when full size, but this will require blocking off the end so that they are unable to eliminate waste in a section and then move to another that is apart from where they soiled.

In summary, per the criteria mentioned above, you need to cordon off the crate to accommodate your puppy's smaller size and then expand it as he or she grows.

"What do I put into the crate?"

Toys, treats, a blanket or mat, and the home furnishings a young puppy needs and desires to be entertained. Avoid televisions, tablets, and radios.

Seriously, you should provide an ample supply of natural material indestructible chew toys, and things such as indestructible balls. All of the chews and toys should be large enough not to be swallowed, and tough enough to withstand being torn apart into smaller portions that can be swallowed by your puppy. Treats will be occasionally required, and stuffing them into the chew toys will occupy the young pup for hours.

Clean water is another essential item that all dogs must have regular access to. You can utilize a small rodent-type water dispenser attached to the side of the crate. If you know that your dog will only be in the crate under 2 hours, then he or she will probably be able to go without water.

"Where do I place the crate?"

It is a good idea to place the crate close to where you are located in the house. This keeps a puppy from feeling lonely and you able to keep an eye out for signs that he or she needs to eliminate waste. After housetraining has been a success, the crate does not have to be located beside you, only near you or in central location to where you are working or relaxing. Eventually the crate can be located at further distances, but you never want your dog to feel isolated.

Introducing Your Dog to the Crate

These steps will help your dog to adjust to his crate and associate it with good things such as security, comfort, and a quiet place to ponder the meaning of life, such as why he or she walks on 4 legs and humans on 2, and how his food magically appears.

Never force your dog into the crate by using physical means of persuasion. Crate training should be a natural process that takes place on your dog's time schedule. Curious dogs might immediately begin to explore the inner domain while others take some time, and possibly some coaxing by using lures such as toys and food. Let the process proceed in small steps and gradually your dog will want to spend more time in his new 5-star luxury crate. This training can proceed very quickly or take days to complete.

Phase I

1. Set the crate in a common area and confirm that all of the crate's goodies are inside. Open and secure the door. If your dog does not mosey over on his or her own accord, then place them near the crate's entrance and give him a pep talk using your happy-go-lucky fun voice. Wait a bit and see if his curiosity kicks in and he begins to explore the inner domain.

2. If your pep talk and shining personality are not sparking his curiosity then go to plan B - food lures. To begin, you don't have to use anything fancy, just use his normal puppy food. Drop some in the back of the crate and a couple closer to the front door, and see if that gets his little tail wagging and paws moving. After you place the food inside, step away and give him some room to make his own decisions. Do not force anything. Just observe him throughout the day and see if your dog is venturing inside or near the crate. Do this a few times throughout the day.

3. If this does not work, try it again. If he is still disinterested, you can also drop a favorite chew toy into the crate and ask him to find his toy and see if that lures him into the crate.

4. Continue doing this process until your dog will walk all the way into the crate to retrieve the food or toy. This step is sometimes accomplished in minutes, but it can also take a couple of days. Be sure to praise your dog for successfully entering it. Do not shut the door. Observe whether they are calm, timid, or frightened.

5. Once your dog is regularly entering his crate without fear, you can move onto phase II.

Phase II

Phase II will help if your dog is not acting as though his crate is a place that he wants to enter and remain inside, and might be showing signs of fear or anxiety when inside. This phase will help warm him up to his crate.

By using feeding time, you can reinforce that the crate is a place that your dog should enjoy. During Phase II training, remain in the presence of your dog's crate or at least in the same room. Later you will begin leaving the room where he is crated.

1. Start by feeding your dog in front of his crate's door. Feeding your dog near his crate will create a nice association with the crate. *If your dog already enters his crate freely, set the food bowl inside so that he has to enter the crate to eat.

2. Next, place his food bowl far enough into the crate that your dog has to step inside to eat. Then each following time that you feed him place the bowl further inside.

3. When your dog will stand and eat inside his crate, and you know that he is calm and relaxed, then you can close the crate's door while he eats his meal.

The first time, immediately after he has finished the meal, open the door. Then after each successive meal, leave the door closed for longer durations. For example, after meals gradually increase the length of time to 2, 3, and 4 minutes and then incrementally increase it further until you reach 10 to 15 minutes. Stay diligent and, if you notice your dog beginning to frantically whine or act anxious, back up and then slow down on the time increases.

4. If your dog continues whining the next time, then leave him in there until he calms down. This is important, because you cannot reinforce that whining is a way out of the crate, or a way to always get your attention or manipulate you.

5. Now that he is comfortable entering, eating, and spending some time in his crate, move onto Phase III, which explains about training your dog to enjoy spending more time in the crate with you around and also out of the house.

Phase III

This is where you will continue increasing the time duration that your dog is crated. First, be certain that he is not displaying signs of fear or anxiety.

Whining and whimpering does not always signify that anxiety is present. It is often a tool used when they want some attention from their mom or people. It is a sympathy tool that is honed when they are weaning on their mother's milk.

If you choose at this point, you can begin issuing a command that goes with your crating action. For example, say "Crate", "Home", "Cage", "Cave", or whatever is simple and natural for you. Maybe cage sounds negative to us, but your dog doesn't know the difference.

1. Stand next to the crate with his favorite toy and then call him over to you and give the command "Cave", while placing the toy inside. A hand signal that you choose can also be used along with this command, but make sure that you do not use the same hand signal for another command. As an option, you can use a favored treat instead of a toy.

When he enters, praise him, shut the door, and let him stay inside for 10 to 15 minutes. You should remain close to the crate. Do this a few times separated by an hour or 2. During dog training, gradually proceeding is always a good rule to follow.

2. Repeat the step above, but this time only stay nearby for about 5 minutes, and then leave the room for an additional 10 to 15 minutes. When you return, do not rush over to the crate, instead remain in the room for a few more minutes and then let your dog out of the crate. It is not necessary to physically remove him, just open the door.

Repeat this 5 to 7 times per day and gradually increase the duration that your dog remains in the crate. Work your way up to 30-40 minutes when you are completely out of sight.

Do not forget to use your vocal command and physical cue every time that you want your dog to enter his crate.

3. Continue increasing the time that he is crated while you are home. Work up to 1 hour.

4. Next, place the crate near your room and let him sleep the night inside the crate near to where you are sleeping such as in the doorway or just outside your bedroom. At this time, if your dog is able to go 2 hours without needing to eliminate, then you can also begin to leave your dog crated when you need to leave the house for short durations of under 2 hours.

A good way to begin is to leave your dog in his crate while you are outdoors doing yard work. Remember that when you return inside to act casual and normal. Do what you need upon returning inside, and then open the crate door and then secure the opened door.

*Puppies usually need to eliminate waste during the night, thus you will need to make some late night trips outdoors.

As your dog becomes accustomed to his crate and surroundings, you can begin gradually to move the crate to your preferred locations, but not to an isolated place.

Tips & Troubleshooting

In the beginning, especially with puppies, keep the crate close to where you are in the house and where you sleep at night. As mentioned, you want to avoid any negative associations such as isolation that can result in depression or contribute to separation anxiety. This also strengthens your bond, and allows easy access for late night elimination trips.

Due to bladder and bowel control, puppies under 6 months should be kept crated for periods under 4 hours.

Ignore whining unless your dog responds to your elimination command or phrase that you have been using when taking him to his elimination spot. If he does respond, then you know that the whining was for that and not simply for attention.

I know it is difficult to ignore whining, but it must be done so that your new dog or puppy understands that you are not at their disposal every time they seek attention. If you are bonding, socializing and practicing the other suggested items, then your puppy or dog should not need the extra attention.

- Before crating, take your dog outdoors to eliminate. There should be only 5-15 minutes between elimination and crating. *This provides the best chance of your dog not soiling his crate.

- Don't forget to leave plenty of fresh water, chew toys and items that require problem solving. Food-stuffed toys are a good choice.

- Don't place your dog into the crate for long periods before your departure from the house. Try to keep it under 15 minutes or less.

- Vary the time between crating and departure.

- When soiling accidents occur inside the crate, thoroughly clean the crate and its contents with a pet odor neutralizer. Warning, do not use ammonia.

- A couple of warnings regarding crating - Avoid crating in direct sunlight or excessive heat, if your dog is sick with diarrhea or vomiting, or is having bowel and urine control issues. You can resume training once these are resolved.

- Always provide sufficient exercise and socialization.

- Never use the crate as a form of punishment.

- Quick review of the approximate crating times per age are as follows: 9-10 weeks, 30-60 minutes; 11-14 weeks, 1-3 hrs; 15-16 weeks, 3-4 hrs; 17 + weeks, 4-6 hrs.

- *To thwart separation anxiety issues, never make a big emotional showing when you leave the house. Always act normal, because it is a normal thing for you to come and go. Do the same when you return, do not over dramatize your return, first do what you need to do and then casually go over to his crate and open the door without making a big show of it. This helps your dog to understand that all of this coming and going is a normal part of his life.

- After your dog is housetrained and is no longer destructive, do not forcibly crate your dog except when you absolutely need him crated. During other times, leave the door securely open and allow him to voluntarily come and go as he chooses.

- Some reasons why your dog might continue to soil his own crate are as follows. The crate is to large, there is a diet issue, health issue, he is too young to have control, is suffering severe separation anxiety, or has drunk to much water prior to crating.

- Another contributing factor could be the manner that your dog was housed prior to your acquiring him. If he was confined continuously in a small enclosure with no other outlet for elimination, this will cause issues with housetraining and crating. If this is true for your dog, training will require more time and patience.

- Separation anxiety is an issue that cannot be solved using a crate. Consult the diagnosing and solving separation anxiety guidelines.

That wraps up crate training. I wish you well with crate and housetraining. I am sure that you will do wonderfully in shaping your dog's behaviors.

14 Teaching Clicker Response

As a reminder before you move forward training, if you are not using a clicker to train your pup, use rewards of treats, praise, toys, play or whatever your pup considers a proper reward for compliance. I have written the following training protocols with clicker training, so ignore the clicker parts and just use rewards.

Most importantly though, your timing needs to be spot-on, just like with the clicker. Marking the exact action you want at the exact time your pup performs it, so it's still a good idea to read through all of the chapters because they contain valuable training advice.

Important - Conceal the treat! <u>Do not show your puppy the treat before depressing the clicker button,</u> and never deliver the treat prior to the clicker emitting a clicking sound. If you do this, your puppy will be responding to the treat and not the click, and this will undermine your training strategy.

Training should begin by simply observing your Mini Aussie puppy. What you are looking for is a desired behavior to reward. In other words, if your puppy is doing anything considered an undesirable behavior, then do not reward him.

As long as your puppy is relaxed and behaving well, you can begin to train him using this clicker response training. What you are doing here is training your puppy to associate the clicker sound with doing something positive. Whenever you click, your puppy will associate the sound with an acceptable performance, and will know that he or she has a reward coming.

Timing is crucial when training your puppy. The essential technique when training your puppy with the clicker is by clicking precisely as the correct action takes place, followed by treating. It does not take long for your puppy to associate their behavior with the clicking sound, and subsequently receiving a treat. Make sure that the treat is produced immediately following the clicking sound.

Note: Throughout this training guide, click and treat is sometimes written as C/T. In addition, for ease of writing, I mostly refer to the gender of your dog as male, even though I know many people have female dogs. Please do not be offended by this.

Crucial – Never click without treating, and never treat without clicking. This maintains the connection and continuity between clicking and treating, which is the framework for achieving your desired outcomes.

Steps

1. When your puppy is relaxed, you should stand, or kneel down at about an arm's length away, and then click and give your puppy a treat.

2. Repeat this clicking and treating about 5-15 times. Pause for several seconds between clicks to allow your puppy to resume whatever he was doing. Do not click and treat if he seems to be begging for another treat. Find times throughout the day when he is performing any desired behavior, then click and treat. This teaches your puppy to associate the click with what you want him to do, and a tasty food treat.

When you click and your puppy's head swings around in anticipation of a treat, then you know that your puppy has made the association between the clicking sound and a reward.

4. Repeat steps 1 and 2 the day following the introduction of clicker training. When your puppy quickly responds to the click, then you can begin using the clicker to train commands.

Teaching puppies to respond to this method can take several training sessions, but most commonly after about a dozen click and treats, they will begin to connect the clicking sound with a treat. Usually, at the end of the first 5-minute session, puppies tend to swing their head around when they hear the clicker sound.

Helpful Hint

After some dedicated training sessions, puppies tend to stop in their tracks and instantly come to you for a treat. At this time refrain from using this clicker technique to get your dog to come to you, but instead follow the instructions for teaching the come command in Chapter 16.

15 Name Recognition

After your puppy responds to the clicking sound, and he knows very well that treats follow the clicking sound, you can now begin teaching him commands and tricks.

Now, we are going to teach your puppy some specific things. Let's start with the fundamental exercise that is teaching your puppy to respond to his or her name. I assume that you have already gone through the painstaking process of naming your puppy, and now when his or her name is spoken you want your puppy to respond. This can be easy, fun and gratifying when you finally achieve positive results.

Teaching your puppy his name is a basic and necessary objective that must be accomplished in order to gain and keep your puppy's attention during further training. This important step is often unrecognized as crucial to dog training; many first-time dog owners don't realize it's separate from training commands.

Before beginning training, be sure to gather an ample variety of treats. Put these treats in your pockets, treat pouch or on a tabletop out of sight, and out of your puppy's reach.

1. Ignore your puppy until he looks directly at you, and when he does, click and treat him. Repeat this 10-15 times. This teaches your puppy to associate the click with a treat when he looks in your direction.

2. Next, when your puppy looks at you, begin adding your puppy's name, spoken right before you click and treat.

3. Continue doing this until your puppy will look at you when you say his or her name.

4. Gradually phase out clicking and treating your puppy every time that he or she looks at you. Gradually decrease C/T incrementally; 1 out of 2 times, then 1 out of 3, 4, and then not at all. Do not phase out the C/T too quickly.

After successful name recognition training, you should C/T on occasion to refresh your puppy's memory and reinforce the association between hearing his name and receiving a treat. Observe your puppy's abilities and pace during this training process and, when needed, adjust appropriately. The ultimate goal is to have your puppy obey all the commands via vocal or physical cues, without a reward.

Responding to his or her name is the most important learned behavior, because it is the foundation skill for all future training. Therefore, you will want to give this training a considerable amount of attention, and thoroughly complete it before moving on. Saying your puppy's name to gain his attention will always prelude issuing commands, e.g. "Axel, come." "Axel, sit."

I advise that you repeat this exercise in various locations inside and outside your home, while he is out on the leash, in the yard or in the park.

Eventually, make sure that you practice this while there are distractions, such as when there are guests present, when his favorite toys are visible, when there is food around and when he is among other dogs.

- Always maintain good eye contact when you are calling your puppy's name. Keep on practicing this name recognition exercise until there is no doubt that when you speak your puppy's name, he or she knows whom you are referring to and they respond appropriately.

It may sound odd, but also try the training when you are in different physical positions, such as sitting, standing, kneeling or lying down. Mix it up so that he gets used to hearing his name in a variety of areas and situations, and repeat this process frequently. No matter the situation, this command must be obeyed.

Name recognition will avoid trouble later on down the line. For example, if your puppy gets into something that he should not, such as a scrap with another dog, chasing a cat or squirrel, or far worse, getting involved in a time-share pyramid scheme, you can simply call your puppy's name to gain his attention and then redirect him.

You invariably want your puppy to come no matter what the distraction, so training "come" is also a crucial command to teach him, and regularly practice this throughout the lifetime of your dog. Remember, your puppy first needs to know his or her name so that you can teach these other commands such as come.

To be certain that you are able to grab your dog's attention in any circumstance or situation, continue to practice this training into adulthood to reinforce the behavior. When your puppy is appropriately responding to his or her name, I recommend moving forward to the come and sit commands.

16 "Come"

After your puppy recognizes, and begins responding to his name being called, then the "Come" command takes priority as the first command to teach. Why? Because this one could save his life, save your sanity and avoid you the embarrassment of running through the neighborhood in the middle of the night wearing little more than a robe and slippers while pleading for your dog to return.

There are quite a few drills and instructions for properly teaching this command but if you follow through completely your dog will obey the come command at least 90% of the time.

If, by chance, he is checking out the olfactory magic of the trash bin, the best way to redirect your dog is firmly command him to "Come", followed immediately by a reward when he complies. Petting, verbal praise or play is an appropriate reinforcement and an effective redirecting incentive during this type of situation.

In order to grab your dog's attention no matter what activity he is engaged in, it is necessary to implement an effective verbal command. Unfortunately, the word "come" is a commonly used word that is spoken regularly during daily life, thus making it difficult to isolate it as a special command word, so I suggest that a unique and infrequently used word be chosen for this.

With my dog Axel, I use "jax" as my replacement word for come. For example, I say "Axel jax", which replaces the standard, "Axel come", or "Axel here". When your dog hears this special cue word, he will recognize it as the word associated with the command to return to you and receive a special treat. However, if you find it effective and natural there is nothing wrong with simply using come as your command word.

Note: Choose a command word with 1 or 2 syllables, and one that you can easily say, because it will be difficult to change the substituted "come" command word later. Examples are crag, cane and here.

When training the come command outside, use a long, check cord leash about 20 feet (six meters) or more, especially when you leave the yard and head to an open field or park. These leashes are also handy for fieldwork, sports and tracking.

Here's what to do-

1. If you have chosen to use a unique come command, you can begin here. We will not use the clicker at this time. First, gather your assortment of treats, such as bits of steak, bacon or whatever your dog most covets.

Begin with the tastiest treat in hand and speak the new command word, immediately followed by the treat. When your dog hears this new word, he will begin to associate it with a special treat. Keep repeating this exercise, and mix up the treats that you provide. Remember to conclude each training session by providing a lot of praise to your dog. Repeat for about 10 repetitions and then proceed to the next step.

2. Gather your clicker and treats, and then find a quiet, low distraction place so that both of you can focus. First, place a treat on the floor and walk to the other side of the room. Next, hold out a hand with a visible treat in it. Now, say your dog's name to get his attention, followed by the command "Come" using a pleasant, happy tone when you do it.

When your dog begins to move towards you, press the clicker and praise him all the way until he reached the treat in your hand. The objective of this is for him to ignore the treat on the ground and come to you. When he gets to you, treat him from your hand and offer some more praise and affection. Be sure to not click again and only give the treat.

Each time your dog comes to you, pet or touch his head and grab a hold of his collar before treating him. Sometimes do this on top of the collar, and sometimes beneath his head on the bottom of the collar. This action gets your dog used to being held, so when you need to grab a hold of him by the collar he will not shy away or fight you. This was covered earlier in the chapter on handling.

Do this 10-12 times, and then take a break. Make sure that your dog accomplishes the task by walking the complete distance across the room to you, while wholly ignoring the treat that you placed on the floor.

Help

If your dog is stopping at the treat on the floor and not coming to you, do not use the clicker or any body movements that can be mistaken for a reward, ignore him.

If your dog can't quite seem to "get it", then reward him when he takes the first few steps toward you and before he gets to the treat. This is shaping your dog's behavior by rewarding partial completion. Next, you want to make sure he comes closer and closer to you before rewarding him until he finally makes it all the way to you. When he does, give him a barnbuster, triple-sized reward.

- For the next session, you will need the assistance of a family member. First, situate yourself at a distance of about 5-6 paces opposite the other person, and place a treat on the floor between the two of you. Both of you should show your dog a treat when you say his name followed by "Come".

Now, take turns calling your dog back and forth between the two of you. Treat and praise your dog each time he successfully comes all of the way to either of you, while ignoring the treat on the floor. Repeat this about a dozen times. The objective of this exercise is to reinforce the idea that coming when commanded is not only for you, but is beneficial to him as well.

- This time, grab your clicker. As before, put a treat on the ground, move across the room, and then call your dog's name to get his attention, but this time hold out an empty hand and give the command. This will mess with him a little, but that's okay, he's learning.

As soon as he starts to come to you, give him praise and, when he reaches you, click and treat by using the opposite hand that you were luring him with. If your dog is not completing the distance to you, press the clicker as he begins to move closer to you, and the first time he completes the distance, give him a supersized treat serving (7-10 treats). Each additional time your dog comes all of the way to you, reward him with a regular-sized treat serving. Do this about a dozen times, and then take a break.

- Keep practicing this exercise, but now call your dog using an empty hand. Using this technique over several sessions and days should eventually result in a successful hand signal command. Following your dog's consistent compliance with this hand signal training, you can then take the training to the next step by phasing out the hand signal by using only a verbal cue. When shifting to the verbal cue training, reduce treating incrementally, first by treating 1 out of 2 times, then 1 out 3 times, followed by 1 out of 4, 5, 6 and, lastly, without treating at all.

Note: It is important to treat your dog periodically in order to reinforce the desired behavior that he is exhibiting as well as complying with the command you are issuing. Make sure your dog is coming when commanded, including when all family members and friends issue the command.

By the end of this section, your dog should consistently be obeying the hand signal and the verbal come commands successfully.

Let's get complex

Now, by adding distractions we will begin to make obeying commands a more difficult task for your dog. The outcome of this training should result in better control over your pooch in times when there are distracting stimuli.

First, find somewhere there are sights, sounds and even smells that might distract your dog. Almost anything will serve as a distraction. You can intentionally implement distractions, such as having his favorite toy in hand, by having another person present, or even doing this training beside the half roast ox that is on the backyard rotisserie.

Indoors, distracting aspects of daily home life, such as cooking, the noise of the television, the doorbell or friends and family coming and going can serve as distractions. Even move to calling your dog from different rooms of the house, meanwhile gradually introducing other distractions, such as music from the stereo, groups of people and combinations of the sort.

Of course, the outdoor world is a megamall of potential interruptions, commotions and interferences for your pal to be tantalized and diverted by.

Hint - During this training exercise, you will find it helpful to keep a log of not only how your dog is progressing, but also accounting for the different kinds and levels of distractions your dog is encountering.

Now, in a high stimulus setting, resume training using the previous set of learned commands. As before, begin with treats in hand, because in this instance, when necessary the snacks will act as a lure for your dog to follow rather than a reward. This will help him focus. The goal is to dispense with the treats by gradually phasing them out, eventually only using the vocal command.

When outdoors with your dog, practice calling the command "Come" when you and your dog are in the yard with another animal or person, followed by increasing and more complex distractions. These distractions could include a combination of a person and animal together, followed by multiple people conversing or having children running around. After this, you can even throw some toys or balls into the distraction mix.

Eventually, move out onto the streets and sidewalks while introducing him to increasingly busier locations, remembering to keep track of your dog's progress as the situations become more and more distracting. The goal is that you want your dog to come every time you call "come", no matter how much noise and movement is happening around him.

If your dog consistently begins to return to you 7 or 8 times out of each 10 commands, regardless of the distractions, this shows that the 2 of you are making very good progress, and that you are well on your way to the ideal goal of 9 out of 10 times. If your dog is managing 10 out of 10 times, you may consider enrolling him at an Ivy League university or paying a visit to NASA, because you've got yourself one special canine there.

We all want a dog that comes when you use the "Come" command. Whether he is 7 houses down the road, or just in the next room, a dog that comes to you no matter what he is engaged in, is a dog worth spending the time training.

Interrupting Fetch Exercises, Hide & Seek, and the Decoy Exercise

Practice all of the following exercises with increasing distractions, both indoors and outdoors. Focus on practicing one of these exercises per session, eventually mixing up the order of the exercises as your dog masters each. Remember it is always important to train in safe areas.

Interrupting Fetch Exercises

Get an ample-sized handful of your Mini Aussie's favorite treat. Then, lob a ball or a piece of food a reasonable distance and, as your dog is in the process of chasing it, call him by issuing the come command. If he comes after he gets the ball/food, give your dog a little reward of one piece of treat. If he comes before he gets the ball/food, give your dog a supersized (7-10) serving of treats.

If your dog is not responding to your come command, then throw the ball and quickly place a treat down towards his nose height while at the same time saying, "Come", and when he comes to you click and give him a supersize treat. Then, begin phasing out the treat lure.

After you have thrown the ball/food over several sessions, it is time to change it up. Like the exercise prior, this time you will fake throwing something and then call your dog. If your dog goes looking for the ball/food before he comes back to you, give him a small treat. If he comes immediately after you say, "Come", give him a supersized treat portion. Repeat this exercise 7-10 times per session.

Hide & Seek

While you are both outside, and your dog is distracted and does not seem to know you exist, quickly hide from him. When your dog comes looking for you, and eventually finds you, click and treat your dog and give him lots of love and praise. By adding a little drama, make it seem like an extremely big deal that your dog has found you. This is something that you can regularly practice and reward.

The Decoy

One person calls the dog; we call this person the trainer. One person tries to distract the dog with food and toys; we call this person the decoy. After the trainer calls the dog, if the dog goes toward the decoy, the decoy person should turn away from the dog and neither of you offer rewards. When the dog goes towards the trainer, he should be rewarded by both the trainer and the decoy. Repeat 7-10 times per session.

Helpful Hints

1. Let your dog know that his coming to you is always the best thing ever, sometimes offering him supersized treat rewards for this behavior. Always reward him by treating or praising, and when appropriate you can add play with a favorite toy or ball.

2. Never call your Mini Aussie for something he might find unpleasant. To avoid this, disguise the real purpose. If you are leaving the field where he has been running, call your dog, put on the leash and play a little more before leaving. If you are calling your dog to get him into the bath, provide a few minutes of affection or play instead of leading him straight into the bath. This will pacify and distract him and prevent him from developing any negative associations in relation to you. *This is worth noting and something many people forget to remain diligent about.

3. You are calling, and your puppy is not responding. What do you do now? Try running backwards away from your dog, crouch, and clap or show your dog a toy or food. When he comes, still reward him even if he has stressed you out. Avoid running towards your dog because it signals play - catch me.

4. If your dog has been enjoying some unabated freedom off his lead, remember to give him a C/T when he checks in with you. Later you can phase out the C/T and only use praise.

5. You should practice the come command 5 to 10 times daily, and keep it ongoing for life. This command is one of those potentially life-saving commands that help with all daily activities and interactions. The goal is that

your dog will come running to you, whether you are in or out of sight, and from any audible distance. As dog owners, we know that having a dog that obeys this command makes dog-related things less stressful.

17 "Drop it"

Teaching your Mini Aussie pup to drop it is a very important step in protecting your dog. Why? Well, if you have ever owned a young puppy, you know that it is one giant mouth gobbling up whatever is in sight. Rumor has it that Stephen Hawking actually got the idea of the black hole from his puppy's ever-consuming mouth.

Joking aside, sometimes valuable and dangerous things go into that all-consuming mouth, and the command to drop it may save a family heirloom, over even perhaps your dog's life.

If you teach your dog correctly, each time you command, "Drop it", your pup will open his mouth and drop whatever is in it. Most importantly, he will not only drop the item, but will allow you to retrieve it without protesting. When teaching the drop it command you must offer a good trade for what your dog has in his mouth. You need to out-treat your dog by offering a better treat of higher value in exchange for what is in his mouth at the time you issue the command.

Importantly, it is a good idea to stay calm and not chase your puppy because this elicits a play behavior that can work against your desired training outcomes.

If this command is successfully taught, your puppy will actually enjoy hearing "drop it". This command will also build trust between the 2 of you. In example, if you say, "Drop it", then you retrieve the item, and afterward you give a treat, he will understand that you are not there simply to steal the thing he has found and is enjoying. This will develop trust and the pup will not guard his favorite toys, food and items such as his dog bowl.

Negative behaviors such as guarding can be avoided with this and other socialization training. Guarding is an aggressive behavior and something that can be avoided by early, proper training practices.

Teach "Drop it" Like This

1. Gather a variety of good treats, and a few items your dog might like to chew on, such as a favorite toy or a rawhide chew. With a few treats in hand, encourage your dog to chew on one of the toys. When the item is in his

mouth, put a treat close to his nose and say, "Drop it". As soon as he opens his mouth, click and treat him as you pick up the item. Then, return the item to your dog.

At this point, your dog may not want to continue to chew on the item because there are treats in the area and his mouth is now free to consume. If he appears now to be distracted by the treats you possess, rather than the chew toy, you can take this as an opportunity to pause the training.

Be sure to keep the treats handy though, because throughout the day when you see him pick something up, you can practice the drop it command. Do this at least 10 times per day or until this command is mastered.

In the event that he picks up a forbidden item (running shoes), which you may not want to give back to your pooch, instead, give your puppy an extra tasty treat or a supersized serving as a fair exchange for the item that you confiscate. You want your puppy to be redirected, and he should be properly rewarded for his compliance.

2. Once you have done the treat-to-the-nose drop it command 10 times, try doing it without holding the treat to his nose. Continue to use your hand, but this time it should be empty. Say the command, and when he drops the item, click and treat.

*Make sure the first time he drops it when you are not holding a treat to his nose, that you give him a supersized treat serving from a different hand.

Practice this over a few days and training sessions. Do not rush to the next step until his response is consistently compliant, and training is successful at a high rate of 85%+.

3. This next part of the drop it training will further reinforce the command, in particular during situations where a tug-of-war between you may ensue. This time you will want to use a treat that your dog might find extra special, like a hard chew toy pig's ear or rawhide, making sure that it is something that cannot be quickly consumed.

Next, hold this new chew toy in your hand and offer it to your dog, but this time do not let it go. When your dog has the chew toy in his mouth, say, "Drop it". When your dog drops it for the first time, C/T, being sure to give your dog extra treats, and then offer the chew toy back for him to keep.

Because better treats are available, he may not take the chew toy back. Recognize this as a good sign, but it also signals a time for a break. Later, repeat this training about a dozen times before you move on to the next phase of teaching drop it. If your dog is not dropping the chew toy after clicking, then the next time use a higher value treat.

4. For the next phase of training, repeat the exercise above, but this time do not hold onto the chew, just let him have it. As soon as your dog has it in his mouth, give the command "Drop it". When your dog drops the chew toy, C/T with a supersized portion, then be sure to give the chew toy back to him to keep. Your dog will be thrilled by this exchange. Once you have successfully done this a dozen times, move onto the next step.

During this phase, if your dog does not drop the toy, it will be necessary to show the treat first, as an incentive. Once he realizes that you have treats, you will want to work up to having him drop it before the treat is given. This is actually bribery, and I do not suggest utilizing this action as a shortcut elsewhere during training. Remember, only use this method as a last resort, and discontinue it quickly.

5. Now, try this command with the things around the house that he is not supposed to chew on, such as pens, chip bags, socks, gloves, tissues, shoes, or that priceless 15th Century Gutenberg bible.

After you and your dog have achieved success indoors with this command, try the exercise outside where there are plenty of distractions. To hold his attention when you are moving into situations that are more distracting, be sure to have with you the best treats.

Keep in mind that your goal is to have the drop it commands obeyed in any situation, so keep increasing the distractions when training.

6. Practice the drop it command when playing fetch, and other games. For example, when your dog returns to you with his ball, command "Drop it", and when he complies, offer up the magic duo of praise plus a treat.

7. Gradually phase out the clicking and treating of your dog every time that he drops something on command. Progressively reduce treating by first treating 1 out of 2 times, then 1 out 3 times, followed by 1 out of 4, 5, 6 and, finally, not at all.

Always remain aware of your dog's abilities, and his individual pace, being sure not to decrease treating too rapidly. The desired outcome of this training is that your dog will obey all commands by a vocal or physical cue, without a reward. As a reminder, occasionally offer a tasty reward to let him know how much you appreciate his obedience.

Know These Things

- If your Mini Aussie already likes to incite games of grab and chase with you, it is best to curb this behavior from the outset by teaching your dog that you will never chase after him if he thieves and bolts. If your dog grabs and runs, <u>completely</u> ignore him. For you to be effective here, it means that you do not indicate your disapproval with any sort of eye contact, body language, or vocalization. He will quickly get bored, and drop the item on his own.

- If your dog refuses to drop an item, you may have to retrieve it manually. You can do this by placing your hand over the top of your dog's muzzle, and with your index finger and thumb placed on either side of the upper lip, firmly pinch into the teeth.

Before utilizing this technique, it is best to attempt to calm your dog's excitement as much as possible. In most cases, your dog will open its mouth to avoid the discomfort, and at that time you can retrieve the item, whatever it may be. This may take a couple of practices to get the correct pressure and the most effective location to apply it, but it works well.

In the rare instance that this fails, you can simply use both hands and try to separate the jaws by slowly pulling, not jerking, the upper and lower jaws apart. Think crocodile handler, minus the severed limbs.

-Another trick for distracting your puppy's attention is rapping your knuckles on a hard surface to emulate a knock at the door. Often, a puppy will want to investigate what he perceives as a guest's arrival, thus dropping whatever is in his mouth to greet the non-existent visitor.

18 Time to Sit

"Sit" is one of the basic commands that you will use regularly with your pup. Teaching your Mini Aussie to sit establishes human leadership by shaping your dog's understanding of who the leader is. This command can also help to curb problem behaviors such as jumping up on people. It can also assist in teaching polite doggy etiquette, particularly, patiently waiting for you, the trusted leader. Teaching your dog to sit is easy, and a great way for you to work on your catalog of essential leadership skills touched upon in previous chapters.

- Preparation, gather treats and then find a quiet place to begin training. Wait until your puppy sits down on his own, and as soon as his fuzzy rump hits the floor, click and treat. Treat your pup while he is still sitting, then promptly get him up and standing again. Continue doing this until your pup immediately sits back down in anticipation of the treat. Each time he complies, be sure to click and treat.

- Next, integrate the verbal command of "Sit". Each time he begins to sit on his own, say, "Sit", then reinforce it with a C/T. From here forward, only treat your pup when he sits after being commanded to do so. Practice for 10-15 repetitions then take a break.

Do These Variations

1. Continue the training by adding the distractions of people, animals and noises to the sessions. As with the come command, you want your dog to sit during any situation that may take place. Practice for at least 5 minutes each day in different locations and places with increasingly more distractions.

2. Run around with your dog while you are playing with one of his favorite toys. After getting him worked up and excited, command your dog to "Sit". When he complies, click and treat your dog.

3. Before going outside, delivering food, playing with toys, giving verbal praise, petting or getting into the car, ask your dog to sit. Having your dog sit before setting his food bowl down is something you can practice every day to help bolster his compliance to the sit command.

4. Other situations where you can practice the sit command can be when there are strangers present or before opening doors for visitors. Having your dog sit before opening the door to guests is a great way to avoid him jumping onto them. Later, add sit-stay.

Other excellent opportunities to practice the sit command is when there is food on the table, when you are barbequing or when you are together in the park.

Keep practicing this command in all situations that you may encounter throughout the day with your dog. I recommend a gradual increase in the level of distractions you expose the pup to during this training. Sit is a powerful and indispensable command that you will utilize throughout the life of your dog. Later, we will add the command of sit-stay in order to keep your dog in place until you release him.

How are things going for you? Are you seeing results and understanding the power of rewards training? I hope that you are and that both you and your dog are enjoying the training and bonding process.

5. It is important eventually to phase out clicking and treating every time your pup obeys the sit command. After his consistent obedience to the command, begin gradually to reduce C/T by treating every other compliance, then once out 3 times, followed by once out of 4, 5, 6 and, then finally, cease.

Be sure to observe your dog's abilities and pace, making sure not to decrease C/T too rapidly. The overall goal of this training is to have your dog obey all commands without a reward, and only by a vocal or physical cue.

6. Take advantage of each day, and the plentiful opportunities you have to practice the sit command.

19 "Leave it"

Keep in mind that leave it and drop it are distinctly different commands. The goal of the leave it command is to steer your Mini Aussie's attention away from any object before it ends up in his mouth, thus making it a proactive command.

A proficiency in this command will help to keep him safe from dangerous items, for example objects like dropped medications, broken glass, trash, wires, chemical-tainted rags or that treasured item you spy your dog about to place into his mouth.

A simple "leave it" command can thwart those especially smelly, frequently dead things that dogs find irresistible and often choose to bring us as offerings of love and affection. We all know that our dogs love to inspect, smell, taste and, in some cases, roll in what they find. You can begin to teach the leave it command as soon as your dog recognizes his own name, e.g. "Axel, Leave it!"

1. Start with a treat in each fisted hand. Let the puppy have a sniff of one of your fists. When he eventually looks away from the fist and has stopped trying to get the treat, click and treat, <u>but treat your dog from the opposite hand that he sniffed</u>. Repeat this exercise until he completely refrains from trying to get the treat from you, as evidenced by showing no interest in your fist.

2. Next, open your hand with the treat, and show him the treat. Close your hand if he tries to get the treat. Do this until he simply ignores the treat in the open hand, known as the decoy hand. When he ignores it, click and give your dog the treat from the other hand. Keep doing this until from the start of the exercise he ignores the treat in the open hand.

When you have reached this point, add the command, "Leave it". Now, open the decoy hand, say, "Leave it" just once for each repetition, and when your dog does, click and treat him using the other hand.

3. Now, put the treat on the floor and say, "Leave it". If he tries to get it, cover it with your hand. When your dog looks away from the treat that is lying on the floor, click and treat your dog using the other hand. Continue

issuing the command leave it until your dog no longer tries to get the treat that is on the floor.

4. For the next exercise, put the treat on the floor and say, "Leave it", and then stand up, Click and treat if he obeys. Now, while on his leash, walk your dog past the treat and say, "Leave it". If he goes for it, prevent this by restraining him with the leash. C/T him only when he ignores the treat. *Increase the length of time between the leave it command and the C/T. This strengthens your pup's dedication to obeying your instructions.

Teaching your dog to leave it using a treat first, will allow you to work up to objects such as toys, animals, pills, spills and even people. Once he gets the idea in his head that leave it means a reward for him, you both can eventually work towards more complex situations involving more difficult to resist items. Begin with a low value item such as a piece of kibble, and then move to a piece of hard-to-resist meat, his favorite toy, another animal and then people.

5. After your dog is successful at leaving alone the treat and other items, take the training outside into the yard, gradually adding people, toys, animals and other hard-to-resist distractions. Next, head to the dog park or any other place with even more distractions.

6. Remember to keep your puppy clear of dog parks until at least after his seventh week, preferably no sooner than his tenth week, and certainly only after his first round of vaccines. Some veterinarians and experts suggest even waiting until after the second round of vaccinations before your dog is exposed to other animals.

Continue practicing daily until your dog has this command down. This is another potential life-saving command that you will use regularly during the life of your dog and gives you peace of mind.

7. At this point, you both can have some real fun. Try placing a dog biscuit on your pup's paw, snout, or head and say, "Leave it". Gradually increase the time that your pup must leave the biscuit in place. Try this when he is in the sitting and other down positions. Have some fun and be sure to reward your dog the biscuit after he leaves it undisturbed. Enjoy!

Gradually phase out clicking and treating your dog every time that on command he obeys leave it. As with prior commands, begin gradually reducing treating to 1 out of 2 times, 1 out 3 times, then 1 out of 4, 5, 6 and, finally, none.

Remember not to decrease it too quickly or it will undermine your training. Keenly observe your dog's abilities and pace at all times. The goal is that your pooch will obey all the commands without a reward, eventually with only a vocal or physical cue.

20 "Down"

Teaching your Mini Australian Shepherd to lie down not only helps to keep him in one spot, but also offers a calming timeout and is a useful intervention to curtail and even prevent barking. When paired with the stay command, you can keep your dog comfortably in one place for long periods.

Down not only protects your dog in potentially hazardous situations, but it also provides you with peace of mind that your dog will remain in the place that you commanded him to stay. This is yet another essential command that you will utilize daily throughout the lifetime of your dog.

Basics

1. Begin training in a quiet place with few distractions and bring plenty of treats. Wait for your dog to lie down of his own free will, and then click and treat while he is in the lying down position. If he does not pop up afterwards, toss a treat to get him up again.

Repeat rewarding the down posture with C/T's until he begins to lie down immediately after he gets the treat. His compliance means that he is starting to understand that good things come to him when he lies down, so in anticipation of this, he lies right back down.

2. Now, augment the training with the addition of the verbal command down. As soon as your dog starts to lie down, say "Down", and click and treat. From here on, only C/T your dog when he lies down after your command.

3. Next, practice this in a variety of areas and in situations with various distractions. Begin the practice indoors, then take it outside into your yard, and then wander into the neighborhood, and beyond. Remain patient in the more distracting locations.

Situations in which to command your dog to lie down could include when there are strangers present, when there is food nearby, or when the stereo or television is on. Anytime you are outdoors barbequing, having a party, in the park and during walking together are excellent opportunities to practice this command.

Maintain diligence with this training, and attempt to find situations of increasing levels of distraction where you might need to use the command down. Remember that consistent compliance is what you are looking for. The power and importance of the down command will prove to be one of the most useful of all to train and maintain during the life of your dog.

After your success with the training of down, you can then move to the combination command of down-stay, which should be trained in order to keep your dog in place until you release him. Imagine the ease and joy when your pooch accompanies you to the local café and lies quietly and obediently at your feet while you drink your morning coffee.

Having an obedient companion is a very attractive and respected attribute of any responsible dog owner.

It is important to monitor and track your partner's progress by taking notes during training, especially as you increase the distractions, highlight where and when more work and attention is needed.

4. Gradually phase out clicking and treating your dog every time that he obeys the down command. Reduce the treats to 1 out of 2 compliances, followed by 1 out of 3, then 1 out of 4, 5, 6 and, finally, stop altogether. Do not decrease the treats too rapidly and be sure to observe your dog's abilities and pace closely. The goal of the training is to have your dog obey all commands with only a vocal or physical cue, without a reward.

Problems Solved

- If your dog will not comply with the down command, you need to return the training to a low distraction area like a bathroom. Unless your dog likes decorative bath soaps or vanity mirrors, there is not much to distract him in a bathroom. Continue the training there until your pup is regularly obeying you and then move to other rooms.

- If your dog does lie down but pops right back up, be sure that you are only treating him when he is in the lying down position. In this way, your dog will sooner understand the correlation between the command, action and the subsequent treat.

21 "Stay"

Stay is perhaps a command that you have looked forward to teaching, after all, it is up there at the top of the list as one of the most useful and used essential commands. This command can be effectively paired with sit and down. With these combination commands under your belt, daily life with your companion will be made easier for the entire family.

Teaching your dog restraint has many practical uses. By reinforcing the wanted behavior of remaining in place, your dog will not end up in potentially dangerous situations such as running out of the door and into the street.

This command also limits the possibility of your dog putting you in embarrassing or inconvenient situations, such as jumping up on people, or chasing the neighbor's pet kangaroo. Furthermore, it is a valuable command that teaches compliance, which facilitates better control of your dog.

Stay not only teaches your dog patience, but also reinforces his understanding of who is in charge of the decision-making. After you have taught your dog sit and down, the stay command should be next on your training agenda because they make for natural pairings.

1. To begin with, find yourselves a quiet, low distraction place, and bring plenty of treats. Give the sit command, and after he obeys, wait 2 seconds before you click and treat. Continue practicing while gradually extending the duration of time between his compliance and his receiving the click and treat, thus lengthening the time he is in the sit position. Work up to 10-15 seconds of sitting before clicking and treating.

2. Next, you can begin to issue the combination sit-stay command, and this time you can add a hand signal to the mix. While you issue the command, the signal can simply be your flat hand directed towards his fuzzy little face at a distance of about 12 inches/30 centimeters.

You can also choose a unique hand signal of your own to use in conjunction with sit-stay, being careful to avoid the use of the middle finger, as not to offend the neighbors or passersby. Continue practicing while increasing the time your pup is in the sit position. Gradually increase the sit-stay time to 1 minute before you C/T.

3. If your dog gets up during this training, it means you are moving too quickly. Try again with a shorter stay time goal, and then slowly increase the time your dog is to remain completely still. Continue practicing until your dog will stay for longer intervals.

*A good way to keep track of your dog's progress through each training session is always to utilize your training log. This is helpful for many reasons, including monitoring his compliance, goals, outcomes and unwanted behaviors.

Now it is time to test your progress.

Say, "Sit-stay", and take a big step away from your dog and then C/T him for his obedience. Keep practicing this until you can take 2 big steps in any direction away from your dog without him moving. *It is essential that you return to treat your dog at the exact spot in which he stayed in place. Refrain from treating him if he rises or if he comes to you.

Keep progressing with this exercise until you can take several steps away, eventually moving completely out of your dog's sight while he stays stationary. Work towards the goal of him staying motionless for 2 full minutes while you are in his sight, followed by an additional 2 minutes that you remain out of his sight.

By gradually increasing the stay-time interval during this training, you reinforce the stay-response behavior to the point that your dog will stay put no matter what is going on. Often dogs will simply lie down after a number of minutes in the stay position. Usually, after about 5 minutes my dog just lies down until I release him.

- Lastly, begin increasing the distractions while practicing all that has been trained up to this point. As previously instructed, begin the practice indoors, outside into the yard, and then move away from the familiarity of your house and neighborhood.

For obvious reasons, be patient in the more distracting locations. It is important to maintain a practice routine of at least 5 minutes per day, particularly in places with increasing distraction. During your training sessions, continue to add other people and animals, all in a variety of noisy and increasingly distracting environments.

The desired outcome of this training is to have a dog that remains in place in any situation that you both may encounter during your life together.

Now, repeat the above steps in order using the command "Down" and "Down-stay".

- Gradually phase out clicking and treating your dog every time that he obeys a command. As previously instructed, phase out treating by reducing it gradually, first by treating 1 out of 2 times, then 1 out 3 times, followed by 1 out of 4, 5, 6 and, then, finally refrain all together. Be sure not to decrease the treats too quickly. Observe and take notes of your dog's abilities and pace.

When finished with this section you should have the commands "Sit-stay" and "Down-stay" regularly obeyed by your dog. Take care not to train both commands in the same training sessions.

Helpful Hints

- Always reward your dog in the location where he has remained in place.

- It is important to refrain from releasing him with a C/T while using the come command. This will invariably confuse the outcome of the training, and diminish the importance of the come command. Keep it clear and simple.

- Note when your dog decides not to participate. It could be that the training is getting too difficult, too quickly. When giving commands to your dog, vary the stay times and locations. Give the little fella a chance to learn at his own pace.

- Practice the command of stay, particularly before he meets a new person. Practice this also before he follows you out of the door, into the car or in the course of feeding before you put down his food bowl.

- If you encounter any difficulties, back up a step or calmly resume later. Be aware that each dog has his own pace of learning, so your ongoing patience is crucial. It is best to simply laugh, smile and roll with your dog's natural abilities while enjoying the process of teaching and learning together. After all, this is all quality time spent while hanging out with your new best friend.

22 Leash Training

Training your Mini Aussie pup to the leash will probably be one of the hardest tasks you will do. Leash training is one of those practices that take a bit more time and effort from both of you. However, in the end it is very rewarding and serves to strengthen the trust and bond between you and your canine.

A leash or lead is simply the rope that tethers you to your companion. Though a strong, good quality and adjustable leash is mandatory, a feature of greater significance is the collar or harness. There is a variety of collars to choose from and it is up to you to do some research to determine which one is the best fit for your dog. Head collars and front attachment harnesses are a couple of choices. Make sure it fits properly, is sized correctly and that your dog is comfortable wearing it.

Keep in mind some general guidelines suggested when choosing a collar. If you are small and your dog is large, or if your dog tends to be aggressive or powerful, you will need to exert the greatest control, so the sensible choice should be a head collar.

Front attachment collars are an excellent choice for any dog or activity. Head and frontal attached collars should be used with leashes with a length of 6 feet (1.82 meters) or less. The reason for maintaining a shorter leash is that a longer lead length could allow a bolting dog to gain enough speed to injure himself when the lead runs out and suddenly becomes taut.

The main goal of leash training is to get your dog to walk beside you without pulling against the leash. An effective method during training is simply to stop moving forward when your dog pulls on the lead, turn, walk the opposite direction, and then when he obediently walks beside you, reward him with treats, praise and affection to reinforce the wanted behavior. The following steps will help you to train your dog to have excellent leash manners. Remember, loose leash walking is the goal!

Before moving forward to the next instructional step below, please make sure that your dog consistently performs the target action of the training step that you are teaching. His consistent compliance is necessary for the success of this training, so do not be inclined to hurry or rush this training.

Walking with You Is a Treat (The Beginning)

Start by donning your dog with a standard harness fastened with a non-retractable leash that is about 10 to 20 feet (3-6 meters) in length. Before starting the training session, remember to load up your pouch or pockets with top-notch treats and head out to the back yard or another familiar and quiet, low distraction outdoor spot. It is best if there are no other animals or people present during this initial phase. You need all of your dog's attention on you.

1. First, decide whether you want your dog to walk on your left or right side. The side you choose is the side that you will treat your dog. When you deliver treats, deliver them from your thigh level. Eventually, your dog will automatically come to that side because that is where the goodies can be found. Later, you can train your dog to walk on either side of you, but for now, stick with one side.

Training from both sides allows you the flexibility to maneuver your dog anywhere, such as out of harm's way, or offers more practical applications like walking on either side of the street.

2. Place a harness on your dog and attach the leash. Begin the training by randomly walking about the yard. When your dog decides to walk along

with you, click and treat on the chosen side, at the level of your thigh. To "walk along with you" specifically refers to an action where your dog willingly joins you in full compliance when you move along, and in a manner without applying any resistance to the lead.

If he continues to calmly walk on the correct side, give him a click and treat with every step or 2 that you take together, thus reinforcing the desired behavior. Keep practicing this until your dog remains by your side more often than not.

At this time, do not worry about over-treating your trainee; you will eventually reduce the frequency of delivery and then eventually phase out treats completely upon his successful mastering of this skill. You can deduct the training treats from the next meal.

3. Repeat ambling around the yard with your pal in tow, but this time walk at a faster pace than your prior sessions together. As before, when your dog decides to walk with you, give him a click and treat at thigh level of the chosen side. Keep practicing this until your dog consistently remains by your side, at this new pace. This leash training should occur over multiple sessions and days.

There is no need to rush any aspects of training. Remember to be patient with all training exercises, and proceed at a pace dictated by your dog's energy level and his willingness to participate.

Eyes On the THIGHS (Second Act)

If you are here, then your next task is to train your dog to consistently walk beside you and not pull you around your yard or explore the end of his lead.

Keep your dog focused on the training at hand. Teaching him that you are in control of the leash is crucial.

This time, start walking around the yard and wait for a moment when your dog lags behind or gets distracted by something. If he is distracted, say, "Let's go", followed by a non-violent slap to your thigh to get his attention. Make sure you use a cheerful voice when issuing this command and refrain from any harsh tactics that will intimidate your pooch, because that can certainly undermine any training.

When he pays attention to you, simply walk away. By doing this, it isolates the cue connected to this specific behavior, thus moving closer to your dog's grasp of the command.

- If your dog catches up with you before there is tension on the leash, click and treat him from the level of your thigh. Click and treat him again after he takes a couple of steps with you, and then continue to reinforce this with a C/T for the next few steps while he continues walking beside you. Remember, the outcome of this training is loose leash walking.

If your dog catches up after the leash has become taut, do not treat him. Begin again by saying, "Let's go", then treat him after he takes a couple of steps with you. Only reinforce with C/T when he is compliant.

- If he does not come when you say, "Let's go", continue moving until there is tension on the lead. At this point, stop walking and apply firm but gentle pressure to the leash. When he begins to come towards you, praise him as he proceeds. When he gets to you, do not treat him, instead say, "Let's go", and begin walking again. Click and treat your dog if he stays with you and continue to C/T your dog for every step or 2 that he stays with you.

Keep practicing this step until he remains at your side while you both walk around the yard. If he moves away from you, redirect him with pressure to the lead and the command cue of "Let's go", followed up by a C/T when he returns to the appropriate position of walking obediently in tandem with you.

Do not proceed forward to subsequent steps of the training until your dog is consistently walking beside you with a loose leash, and is appropriately responding to the let's go command. It can sometimes take many days and sessions for your dog to develop this skill, so it is important for you to remain patient and diligent during this time. The outcome of this training is well worth your time and effort.

Oh! The Things to Smell and Pee On (Third Act)

Just like you, your dog is going to want to sniff things and eliminate. During these times, you should be in control. While your dog is on the leash, and when he is in anticipation of his regular treating, or at about each 5-minute interval, say something like, "Go sniff", "Go play", "Free time", or some other verbal cue that you feel comfortable saying, followed by some free time on the leash.

Keep in mind that this is a form of reward, but if he pulls on the leash, you will need to redirect with a "Let's go" cue, followed by your walking in the opposite direction, quickly ending his free time. If your dog remains compliant, and does not pull on the leash before the allotted free time has elapsed, you are still the one that needs to direct the conclusion of free leash time by saying, "Let's go", coupled with you walking in the opposite direction.

Where's Is My Human? (Fourth Act)

Using steps 1 through 3, continue practicing leash walking in the yard. During the course of the training session, gradually shorten the lead until a 6-foot (1.8 meter) length remains. Now, change the direction and speed of your movements, being sure to click and treat your pup every time he is able to stay coordinated with the changes you implement.

As loose-leashed walking becomes routine and second nature for your companion, you can start phasing out the click and treats. Reserve the C/T for situations involving new or difficult training points, such as keeping up with direction changes or ignoring potential distractions.

Out In the Streets (Fifth Act)

Now, it is time for the big step, taking your dog out of the yard and onto the sidewalk for his daily walk. You will use the same techniques you used in your yard, only now you have to deal with more distractions.

Distractions can come in all forms, including other dogs, friendly strangers, traffic, alarming noises, sausage vendors, feral chickens, taunting cats and a host of other potential interruptions and disturbances. At this time, you might want to consider alternate gear, such as a front attachment harness or a halter collar that fits over the head, offering ultimate control over your companion.

Arm yourself with your dog's favorite treats, apply the utmost patience, and go about your walk together in a deliberate and calm manner. Remember to utilize the "Let's go", command cue when he pulls against his leash or forgets that you exist.

In this new setting, be sure to treat him when he walks beside you and then supersize the portions if your dog is obedient and does not pull on the lead during a stressful moment or an excitable situation. Lastly, do not forget to reward him with periodic breaks for sniffing and exploring. The free time rewards will reinforce his willingness to comply.

Stop and Go Exercise (Sixth Act)

Attach a 6-foot lead to the collar. With a firm hold on the leash, toss a treat or toy about 20 feet (6 meters) ahead of you and your dog, then start walking toward it. If your dog pulls the leash and tries to get at the treat, use the let's go command and immediately walk in the opposite direction of the treat. If he stays beside you without struggle while you walk toward the treat, allow him to have it as a reward.

Practice this several times until your dog no longer pulls towards the treat and stays at your side waiting for you to make the first move. The other underlying goal is that your dog should always look to you for direction and follow your lead before taking an action such as running after a toy while still leashed.

Switching Sides (Seventh Act)

After your dog is completely trained to the specific side, and with a few months of successful loose-leash walking practice under your belt, you can begin the training again. This time you will target the opposite side to the one the 2 of you have previously trained.

There is no need to rush, so proceed with the training at the opposite side when you know the time is right, and you are both comfortable with changing it up a bit. As previously mentioned, the desired target is a dog that is able to walk loose leashed on either side of you. This skill is essential for navigating your dog with ease and safety while in the outside world.

Troubleshooting

- If your dog happens to cross in front of you during your time together, he may be distracted, so it is important to make your presence known to him with a gentle leash tug or an appropriate command.

- If your dog is lagging behind you, he might be frightened or not feeling well, so instead of pulling your dog along, give him a lot of support and encouragement. If the lagging is due to normal behavioral distractions, such as scent sniffing or frequent territorial marking, keep walking along. In this case, it is appropriate to pull gently on the leash to encourage him to refocus on the task at hand.

- The reinforcement of wanted behaviors necessitates you delivering numerous rewards when your dog walks beside you or properly executes what it is you are training at that time. During your time together, pay close attention to your dog's moods, patterns and behaviors. You want to pay close attention to these things so that you can anticipate his responses, modify your training sessions, or simply adapt whatever it is you are doing to assure that his needs are being met and you are both on the same page.

Being conscious of your dog's needs assists in maintaining a healthy, respectful bond between the two of you. Make an effort to use playful tones in your voice with a frequent "Good dog", followed by some vigorous petting or some spirited play. Try to be aware of when your dog is beginning to tire and always attempt to end a training session on a high note, with plenty of treats, play and praise.

Heel

You will find this command indispensable when you are mobile, or perhaps when you encounter potentially dangerous situations. There will be times where you will need to issue a firm command in order to maintain control of your dog to keep the both of you out of harm's way. Heel is that command.

During your time together exploring the outside world, things such as another aggressive dog, busy traffic, construction sites, teasing cats or that irresistible squirrel may warrant keeping your dog close to you. If trained to the heel command, your dog will be an indispensable asset in helping to avert possible hazardous circumstances with these examples. The heel command is a clear instruction trained to ensure that your dog remains close beside you until you say otherwise.

- Begin this training inside your back yard or in another low distraction area. First, place a treat in your fist on the side you've decided to train him on. Let him sniff your fist, then say, "Heel", followed by taking a few steps forward, leading him along with the fisted treat at thigh level. Click and treat him as he follows your fist with his nose. The fist is to keep your dog close to you. Practice for a few sessions.

- Next, begin the training as before, but now with an empty fist. With your fist held out in front of you, give the heel command, and then encourage your dog to follow by your side. When he follows your fist for a couple of steps, click and treat him. For each subsequent session, repeat this practice a half dozen times or more.

- Continue to practice heel while you are moving around, but now begin to increase the length of time before you treat your dog. Introduce a new direction in your walking pattern or perhaps use a serpentine-like maneuver snaking your way around the yard. You will want to continuously, but progressively, challenge him in order to advance his skills and to bolster his adaptability in various situations.

During all future outings together, this closed, empty fist will now serve as your non-verbal physical hand cue instructing your dog to remain in the heel position. From here on out, remember to display your closed empty fist at your side when you issue your heel command.

- Now, move the training sessions outside of the security of your yard. The next level of teaching should augment his learning by exposing him to various locations with increasingly more distractions. The implementation of this new variation in training is done to challenge and to enhance your walking companion's adaptability to a variety of situations and stimuli.

Continue to repeat the heel command each time you take your dog out on the leash. Keeping his skills fresh with routine practice will ease your mind when out exploring new terrain. Knowing that your dog will be obedient and will comply with all of your commands, instructions and cues will be satisfying and keep you both safe and sane.

Out in the crazy, nutty world of ours there are plenty of instances when you will use this command to avoid unnecessary confrontations or circumstances with potentially dangerous outcomes. If by chance you choose to use a different verbal cue other than the commonly used heel command, pick a word that is unique and easy to say, and does not have a common use in everyday language. This way you avoid the possibility for confusion and misunderstanding.

23 Teaching "Touch"

Touch has an easy rating and requires no knowledge of other tricks, but your dog should know its name, and sitting on command is helpful. The supplies needed are a wooden dowel to be used as a touch-stick, your clicker, and some treats.

Touch training teaches your dog to touch, and in this lesson to touch the end of a stick. It can be any type of wooden dowel, cut broom handle or similar, which is around 3 feet (1 meter) in length. During training, add a plastic cap, rubber ball, or good ol' duct tape to the end so that there are no sharp edges that can harm your dog. A good sanding job to dull all sharp edges will work as a good alternative.

Teaching "touch" using the touch-stick will enable you to train other tricks. You will discover that the touch-stick is useful in training, so take care that you correctly train your dog the touch command. Touch is used later to teach learn names, ring bell, jump over people, spin, jump, and more.

1. Begin training in a quiet place with few distractions, and bring plenty of treats.

2. Start with your dog in the sitting position or standing near you with his attention towards you. Hold your stick away from your body. Keep holding it while doing nothing else but holding the stick steady at a level that your dog can easily touch with his nose.

3. Luckily, a dog's natural curiosity will get the best of them and your dog should touch the stick. When your dog touches it with his nose or mouth, click and treat. Be sure to click immediately when your dog touches the end of the stick. Sometimes it is just a sniff, but those count for beginning to shape the command and require a C/T to let your dog understand what behavior you are seeking.

If your dog is not interested in the stick, then you will need to do the touching for him. Do this by gently touching your dog's nose while simultaneously clicking, and then treating. Keep doing this until your dog is regularly touching the stick when you hold it out.

4. The next time your dog touches the stick C/T while simultaneously saying the command, "Touch". Remember timing is important in all tricks. Your dog needs to know the exact correct action that he is being rewarded for performing. Repeat this a dozen times. Continue over multiple sessions until your dog is easily touching the end of the touch-stick when commanded. Feel free to add some "Good dog" praises.

Hands On

Teaching Axel this trick was an interesting outing. When I first held out the stick, Axel swiped it away with his paw. After a couple more times, he finally smelled the end with his nose and I quickly clicked and treated him. He responded to that, and after reinforcing that with several more click and treats, he started quickly touching the end of the stick.

After using the touch command a dozen times, he realized a treat came after he touched the end of the stick, and moving forward through a few training sessions, he started touching it each time I issued the touch command. I kept practicing and, after a couple more sessions, I locked it in. I was then able to use the touch command and touch-stick to train other tricks.

If your dog is touching the end of the stick with heavy force, then you can add some foam to the end of the stick to cushion his super-nose.

Troubleshooting

"What if my dog is touching the middle of the stick, or not touching the stick at all?"

I mentioned that Axel took a few swipes at the end of the stick before touching it. Each time he did this, I ignored this behavior, even though he looked at me expecting a reward. He could smell the treats in my hand, but I did not click and reward the wrong action. Finally, as I held the stick out close to his snout, he smelled it with his nose and I quickly clicked and treated.

Do not reward him until your dog is touching only the end of the stick. This allows you to use the touch command to train other tricks. If your dog will not touch it try gently touching the end of the stick to his nose and then C/T, but quickly move away from that and let your dog begin to do the touching on his own.

24 Teaching to Learn Names

Learning names has a medium to hard difficulty rating and requires knowledge of the touch command. The supplies needed are a toy, treats and your clicker.

Dog owners have known for years that dogs are smarter than many people give them credit for. They are capable of learning the names of many different objects, such as their toys, people and places.

Dogs are capable of learning hundreds if not thousands of words. Furthermore, once your dog learns the name of something, he or she can find it, grab it and bring it to you.

Not all dogs are capable of learning the same number of words and some will learn and retain names better than others, so do not get frustrated if it takes some time for your dog to recognize and remember what object, place, or person goes with the name you are speaking.

Using the steps in this exercise your dog can learn the names of all your family members, and his personal items, such as his crate, collar, toys and leash. Beyond those items, your dog can learn the names of different rooms, which enables you to use the go command to have your dog go to a specific room.

Select a toy that you may already refer to by name. Chances are that you already often speak the names of dog-associated items when speaking to your dog and he recognizes that word. Be consistent in your name references to your dog's toys, such as Frisbee®, tug, ball, rope and squeaky. Changing the reference name will sabotage this training.

1. To begin, find a low distraction area, have treats at the ready and one of your dog's favorite toys. I will use tug in this example.

2. Start by using touch and have your dog touch your empty hand, when he does, click and treat your dog. Repeat this 5 times.

3. Next, grab your dog's toy and say, "Touch", and if he touches the tug and not your hand, C/T your dog.

4. Repeat number 3, but this time, add the toy's name, say, "Touch tug". When your dog touches the tug, and nothing else, C/T at the exact moment he does this. Repeat this 6-10 times.

5. After a break, practice steps 1-4 over a few sessions and 2 days.

6. In the next phase warm up with numbers 1-4, then hold the tug out away from you and say, "Touch tug", and when he does C/T. Repeat this 6-10 times. Then extend the tug to arm's length from you and repeat 6-10 times. Practice this over a couple of sessions. Take note of your dog's progress and, when he is ready, proceed to number 7.

7. Now, place the tug onto the floor but keep your hand on it and say, "Touch tug", and when he does, C/T. Repeat 6-10 times.

8. Place it on the floor without your hand on it and say, "Touch tug", and when he does, give him a barnbuster-sized treat serving. Feel free to throw in some verbal good boy/girls. If your dog is not moving to it, be patient, silent and still to see if he can figure it out on his own. Remember that your dog wants his treat.

9. Moving forward with the same toy, place it around the room in different areas increasingly further from you. Place it on top of a small stool, on the ground, low-lying shelves and have your dog touch tug. Practice this over a few days and when your dog is regularly responding move onto number 10 and a new toy.

10. Changing to another toy, use one such as a Frisbee® or a ball, so when it is spoken it sounds very different from the previous toy's name. Repeat the steps 4-9 with this next toy.

11. Time to test if your dog can tell the difference. Sit down on the couch or floor and place both the Frisbee® and the tug behind you. Take out the Frisbee® and practice 5 touches, C/T each time your dog correctly touches on command. Next, do the same with the tug.

12. Now, hold one toy in each hand and say, "Touch Frisbee®" and see if your dog touches the correct toy. If your dog touches the Frisbee®, C/T, and then give him a barnbuster-sized reward. If your dog begins to move towards the Frisbee®, but you observe that he is unsure what to do, C/T for moving in the correct direction. If your dog goes to the tug or does nothing, remain neutral and offer no C/T or verbal reward.

Keep working on this and practicing until your dog regularly goes to the correct toy that you command to be touched. Then following the same process continue adding toys. When you get to 3 and then 4 toys/objects, you can lay all 4 in front of you and command, "Touch (object name)" and see if your dog can choose and recognize the correct toy/object.

13. Practice the touch tug, ball, Frisbee or chew by placing the objects in different parts of the room and have him identify each correctly. Practice this often to keep the names fresh in your dog's mind.

14. Teaching the names of people is done a little differently, because for obvious reasons you cannot hold them in your hand, but if they are willing, you could however have them sit on the floor. You can use the training stick from teaching touch to help teach the names of rooms and things, such as crate, bed and mat. Also, use the training stick to introduce people and their names.

Alternative to #14 - Teaching a person's name to your dog can be taught like this.

1. Hold onto your dog's collar and have a family member show your dog a treat. Have the person walk into the other room. Then say, "Axel, find Michelle", or whatever the person's name is. Now let go of the collar and see if your dog will go into the other room and to that person. It is okay to follow your dog. If he does go to the person, give your dog a C/T and a huge barnbuster reward along with praise.

2. Repeat 5 times and take a break.

3. After number 2, have the family member go into different rooms, and do 5 repetitions in each room.

4. It will take a few sessions for your dog to learn and retain the names. Do not forget to practice throughout his life.

Hands On

I taught this to Axel, but my wife's Poodle Roxie knows many more names of objects, people and places, but Axel can respectably perform the trick. He is my pal and goes through all of these things willingly, but some days I have to give him a break because darn it he earns it.

Teaching Axel names while using the touch command I started out by using the touch command with my empty hand and getting a peculiar look from him. He touched my hand and I gave him a C/T about a half dozen times.

Holding Axel's attention while in the sitting position in front of me, I then picked up the tug and repeated the exercise saying, "Touch tug", and only used C/T when he touched the tug. I'll confess it took a few attempts and I had to adjust my hand so that he had to touch the tug when he moved his nose towards my hand.

I ran through exercises 1-4 over a few days and about 6 sessions.

Eventually, I felt confident to start moving the tug further from my body and then onto the floor, couch cushion, into the corner of the room and so forth. It took some time and patience for him to understand that he was to go to the item being named.

Eventually, I was able to place it into different rooms inside the house and say, "Touch tug" and he would bolt off looking for it. From there I added further toys, such as Frisbee®, that I discovered by his ears and the way that he looked at me that he already recognized the word.

Troubleshooting

"I am scratching my head because my dog does not understand what I am trying to teach!"

In the beginning, you can try maneuvering your hand so that your dog will touch the toy and not your hand.

Watch your time when training. Keep your sessions short and if your dog is still a puppy or acting like one keep your sessions around 3-5 minutes, while older dogs can usually go about 10 minutes per training session. If you notice any signs of fatigue, end the session on a high happy note and stop for the day. Begin anew the following day.

Hint: After your dog recognizes, and is regularly touching objects in different locations, solicit other people to practice giving your dog the command. Combine this with "Take it" and "Bring it" and your dog will go to find and bring to you any objects he has learned the names of. Have fun and enjoy adding objects and people.

25 Go West Young Mini Aussie

"Go" is a great cue to get your puppy into his crate or onto his mat or rug, and later his stuffed goose down micro-fiber plush bed. This is a very handy command to send your dog to a specific location and keep him there while you tend to your business. Before teaching go, your dog should know his name and already be performing to the commands down and stay.

While training the following steps, do not proceed to the next step until your dog is regularly performing the current step.

- Find a quiet, low distraction location to place a towel or mat on the floor and grab your treats. Put a treat in your hand and use it to lure your dog onto the mat while saying, "Go". When all 4 paws are on the mat, click and treat your dog. Do this about 10 to 15 times.

- Start the same way as above, say "Go", but this time have an empty hand, and act as though you have a treat in your fist while you are luring your dog onto the mat. When all 4 paws are on the mat, click and treat your dog. Do this 10 to 15 times.

- Keep practicing with an empty hand and eventually turn the empty hand into a pointed index finger. Point your finger towards the mat. If your dog does not understand, walk him to the mat and then click and treat. Do this about 10 to 15 times.

- Now, cue with "Go" while pointing to the mat, but do not walk to the mat with him. If your dog will not go to the mat when you point and say the command, then keep practicing the step above before trying this step again. Proceed to practicing the command go while using the pointed finger and when your dog has all 4 paws on the mat, click and then walk over and treat him while he is on the mat. Do this about 10 to 15 times.

- Now, grab your mat and try this on different surfaces and other places, such as grass, tile, patio, carpet and in different rooms. Continue to practice this in more and more distracting situations and don't forget your towel or mat. Take the mat outdoors, to your friends' and families' houses, hotel rooms, the cabin and any other place that you have your trusted companion with you.

One Step Beyond – "Relax"

In accordance with go, this is an extra command you can teach. This is a single word command that encapsulates the command words go, down, and stay all into one word. The purpose is to teach your dog to go to a mat and lie on it until he is released. This is for when you need your dog out from under your feet for extended lengths of time like when you are throwing a party.

Pair it with down and stay so your dog will go the mat, lie down, and plan on staying put for an extended period of time. You can substitute it your own command, such as "Settle", "Rest", or "Chill", but once you choose a command stick with it and remain consistent.

This command can be used anywhere that you are, informing your dog that he will be relaxing for a long period and to assume his relaxed posture. You can train this command when your pup is young and it will benefit you throughout your life together.

- Place on the floor your mat, rug, or whatever you plan on using for your dog to lie down on.

- Give the "Go" command and C/T your dog when he has all 4 paws on the mat. While your dog is on the mat, issue the command "Down stay", and after compliance go to him and C/T while your dog is still on the mat.

- Now, give the relax command and repeat the above exercise with this relax command. Say, "Relax", and "Go" and C/T your dog when he has all 4 paws on the mat. While your dog is on the mat, issue the command "Down stay", and C/T while your dog is still on the mat. When your dog understands the relax command it will incorporate go, down, and stay.

Practice 7-10 times per session until your dog is easily going to his mat, lying down, and staying in that position until you release him.

- Next, give only the relax command and wait for your dog to go to the mat and lie down before you click and treat your dog. Do not use any other cues at this time. Continue practicing over multiple sessions, 7-10 repetitions per session until your dog is easily following your 1-word instruction of relax.

- Now begin making it more difficult; vary the distance, add distractions and increase the times in the relax mode. This is a wonderful command for keeping your dog out of your way for lengthy durations. You will love it when this command is flawlessly followed.

Helpful Hint

-While you are increasing the time that your dog maintains his relaxed position, click and treat him every 5-10 seconds.

- You can also shape this command so that your dog assumes a more relaxed posture than when you issue down stay. When your dog realizes that the relax command encompasses the super relaxed posture that he would normally use under relaxed conditions, he will understand that he will most likely be staying put for a lengthy period and he might as well get very comfortable.

Another obedience command that can and should be taught is the release command. Do not forget to teach a release command word to release your dog from any previous command. Release is command #14 in my 49 ½ Dog Tricks book that will soon be, or is already, for purchase. Release is easier to train if your dog already sits and stays on command.

This command informs your dog that they are free to move from whichever previous command you issued and he complied, such as sit or down.

When released, your dog should rise from the position but remain in place. This is an obedience command that can keep your dog safe and you from worrying about your dog bolting off or moving at the wrong time during a potentially dangerous situation. You can choose any command, such as move or break. As a reminder, 1 or 2 syllable words work best when teaching dogs commands.

26 Jumping Issues

Your dog loves you and wants as much attention from you as possible. The reality is that you are the world to your dog. Often when your dog is sitting quietly, he is easily forgotten. When he is walking beside you, you are probably thinking about other things, such as work, dinner, the car, the chores you need to accomplish or anything but your loyal companion walking next to you.

Sometimes your dog receives your full attention only when he jumps up on you. When your dog jumps up on you, then you look at him, physically react in astonishment, maybe shout at him and gently push him down until he is down on the floor. Then, you ignore him again, and make a mental note to teach your dog not to jump up onto you. What do you expect? He wants your attention. Teaching your dog not to jump is essentially teaching him that attention will come only if he has all 4 paws planted firmly on the ground.

It is important not to punish your dog when teaching him not to jump up on you and others. Do not shout "No!" or "Bad!" Do not knee your dog or push him down. The best way to handle the jumping is to turn your back and ignore your dog.

Remember, since he loves you very much, your dog or puppy may take any physical contact from you as a positive sign. You do not want to send mixed signals; instead, you want to practice completely ignoring him, which consists of not looking or speaking to him. If you do use a vocal command, do not say, "Off", instead use "Sit", which your dog has probably already learned. Try not to use a command, and instead proceed to ignore him.

For jumping practice, it would be ideal if you could gather a group of people together who will participate in helping you to train your dog that jumping is a no-no. You want to train your dog to understand that he will only get attention if he is on the ground. If groups of people are not available, then teach him to remain grounded using his family. When your dog encounters other people, use a strong sit stay command so he keeps all 4 paws planted firmly on the ground. I covered sit stay above, and now you understand how useful and versatile this command can be.

No Jumping On the Family

This is the easiest part, because the family and frequent visitors have more chances to help your dog or puppy to learn. When you come in from outside and your dog starts jumping up, say, "Oops!" or "Whoa", and immediately leave through the same door. Wait a few seconds after leaving and then do it again. When your dog finally stops jumping on you as you enter, give him a lot of attention.

Ask the rest of the family to follow the same protocol when they come into the house. If you find that he is jumping up at other times as well, like when you sing karaoke, walk down the hallway or cook at the barbeque, just ignore your dog by turning your back and put energy into giving him attention when he is sitting.

No Jumping on Others

Prevention is of utmost importance and the primary focus in this exercise. You can prevent your dog from jumping by using a leash, a tieback, crate, or gate. Until you have had enough practice and your dog knows what you want him to do, you really should use one of these methods to prevent your dog from hurting someone or getting an inadvertent petting reward for jumping. To train, you will need to go out and solicit some dog training volunteers and infrequent visitors to help.

- Make what is called a tieback, which is a leash attached to something sturdy, within sight of the doorway but not blocking the entrance and which keeps your dog a couple of feet or about a meter away from the doorway. Keep this there for a few months during the training period until your dog is not accosting you or visitors. When a guest arrives, hook your dog to the secure leash and then let the guest in.

Guests Who Want to Help Train Your Dog (Thank You in Advance)

All of this training may take many sessions to complete, so remain patient and diligent during training and prevention until your dog complies with not jumping on people.

- Begin at home, and when a guest comes in through the door, and the dog jumps up, they are to say "Oops" or "Whoa", and leave immediately. Practice this with at least 5 or 6 different visitors, each making multiple entrances during the same visit. If your helpers are jumped on, have them completely ignore your dog by not making any eye or physical contact or speaking anything other than the initial vocal word towards your dog, then have them turn their backs and immediately leave.

- When you go out onto the streets, have your dog leashed. Next, have your guest helper approach your dog. If he strains against the leash or jumps have the guest turn their back and walk away. When your dog calms himself and sits, have the guest approach again.

Repeat this until the guest can approach, pet and give attention to your dog without your dog jumping up. Have the volunteer repeat this at least 5 to 7 times. Remember to go slowly and let your dog have breaks. Keep the sessions in the 5-7 minute range. For some dogs, this type of training can get frustrating. Eventually, your dog will understand that his jumping equals being ignored.

- Use the tie-back that you have placed near the door. Once your dog is calm, the visitor can greet your dog if they wish. If the guest does not wish to greet your dog, give your dog a treat to calm his behavior. If he barks, send your dog to his gated time-out area.

The goal is that you always greet your guests first, not your dog. Afterward, your guests have the option to greet or not greet your dog, instead of your dog always rushing to greet every guest. If he is able to greet guests calmly while tied back, then he may be released. At first hold the leash to see how your dog reacts, then if he is calm release him.

A Caveat to These Two Methods

1) For those who are not volunteers to help teach your dog and are at your home visiting, there is another method. Keep treats by the door, and as you walk in throw them 7 to 9 feet (2.1 - 2.7 meters) away from you. Continue doing this until your dog begins to anticipate this.

Once your dog is anticipating treats every time someone comes through the door it will keep him from accosting you or the visitors that walk through the doorway. After your dog eats his treat and has calmed down, ask him to sit, and then give him some good attention.

2) Teach your dog that a hand signal such as grabbing your left shoulder means the same as the command sit. By combining the word sit with a hand on your left shoulder, he will learn this. If you want to use another physical cue, you can substitute this with your own gesture, e.g. holding your left wrist or ear.

Ask the guests that have volunteered to help train your dog to place their right hand on their left shoulders and wait until your dog sits before they pet him or give any attention. Training people that meet your dog will help both you and your dog in preventing unwanted excitement and jumping up.

Having your dog sit before he can let loose with jumps is proactive jumping prevention.

27 Excessive Barking

Any dog owner knows that dogs bark for many reasons, most commonly for attention. Your Mini Aussie may bark for play, attention or because it is close to feeding time and he wants you to feed him. Dogs also bark to warn intruders and us, so we need to understand why our dog is barking. Not all barking is bad. Some dogs are short duration barkers while others can go on for hours, we do not want that and neither do our neighbors so let's remedy that before it gets out of control.

Whatever the case do not give your dog attention for barking. Do not send the signals that your dog's barking gets an immediate reaction from you, such as you coming to see why he is barking or even moving towards him.

As I mentioned in the opening paragraph, they do sometimes bark to warn us, so we should not ignore all barking but instead we need to assess the barking situation before dismissing it as nonsense barking. With a bit of assessment, you can diagnose your dog's barking and then take the proper action to shape his or her barking behavior.

When you know the cause is a negative behavior that needs correction, say, "Leave it" and ignore him. While not looking at your dog go to the other side of the room or into another room, you can even close the door behind you until your dog has calmed down. *Make it clear to your barking dog that his barking does not result in any rewards or attention.

In everyday life, make sure you are initiating activities that your dog enjoys and are always happening on your schedule. You are the alpha leader so regularly show your pup who is in charge and make sure that he earns what is provided. Have your pup sit before he gets any reward.

I love dogs and I am sure that you do too, but a dog that barks incessantly can drive anyone to frustration and potentially anger. People would be surprised how many dogs have lethal action taken against them from neighbors that have been pushed to the breaking point by a neighbor's unstoppable barking dog. This is something I never want to happen to your family.

Your dog may bark when seeing or hearing something interesting. Below are a few ways to deal with this issue.

Prevention when you are at your residence

1. Teach your dog the command quiet. When your dog barks, wave a piece of food in front of his nose at the same time you are saying, "Quiet". When he stops barking to sniff, click and treat him right away. Do this about 4 or 5 times and then the next time he barks, pretend you have a piece of food in your hand next to his nose and say, "Quiet". Always click and treat him as soon as he stops barking and continue to click and treat him again for every few seconds that he remains quiet after you issued the command.

Eventually, as you make your way to 5 or 10 seconds, gradually increase the time duration between the command quiet, clicking and treating.

2. Prevent it. Block the source of the sound or the sight so that your dog is unable to see or hear the catalyst that is sparking his barking. Use a fan, stereo, TV, curtains, blinds or simply put him in a different area of the house to block him from the stimulus.

3. When your pup hears or sees something that would typically make him bark and he does not bark, reward him with attention, play or a treat. This is reinforcing and shaping good behaviors instead of negative behaviors. This is an important step in reward-based training and shaping non-barking behavior.

The Time Out

Yes, you can use a time out on your dog, but do not use it too often. When you give your dog a time out, it takes your dog out of his social circle and provides your dog with what is known as a negative punishment.

This kind of punishment is powerful and can have side effects that you do not want. Your dog may begin to fear you when you walk towards him, especially if you have the irritated look on your face that he recognizes as the time-out face. The time out should be used sparingly. Instead, focus on teaching your dog the behaviors that you prefer while preventing the bad behavior through blocking the stimulus.

Choose a place where you want the time-out spot to be located. Make sure that this place is not the elimination spot, crate or his play area. Ideally, it will be a boring place that is somewhere that is not scary or too comfortable, but is safe. A gated pantry or the bathroom works well.

- Secure a 2-foot piece of rope or a short leash to your puppy's collar. When your pup barks, use a calm voice and give the command, "Time out", then take the rope and walk him firmly but gently to the time-out spot. Leave him there for about 5 minutes, or longer if necessary.

Release him when he is calm and not barking. You may need to do this 2 to a dozen times before he understands which behavior has put him into the time-out place. Almost all dogs are social and love being around their humans, so this can have a strong impact.

Prevention when you are away from your residence

1. Again, prevent barking by blocking the sounds or sights that are responsible for your dog or puppy going into barking mode. Use a fan, stereo, curtains or blinds, or keep him in another part of the house away from the stimulus.

2. Use a citronella spray collar. Only use this for when the barking has become intolerable. Do not use this when the barking is associated with fear or aggression. So that your dog understands how it works, you will want to use this a few times when you are at home before using it when away.

Citronella collars work like this: The collar has a sensitive microphone that senses when your dog is barking, and when this happens it triggers a small release of citronella spray into the area above a dog's nose. It surprises the dog and disrupts barking by emitting a smell that dogs dislike.

Out walking

While you are out walking your dog, out of shear excitement or from being startled, your pup might bark at other dogs, people, cars and critters. This can be a natural reaction or your dog may have sensitivities to certain tones, the goal is to try to limit the behavior and quickly cease the barking.

Here are some helpful tools to defuse that behavior.

1. Teach your dog the watch me command. Begin this training in the house in a low distraction area. While you hold a treat to your nose, say your dog's name and "Watch me". When your dog looks at the treat for at least 1 second give him a click and treat. Repeat this about 10-15 times. Then increase the time that your dog looks at you to 2-3 seconds and then repeat a dozen times.

2. Next, repeat the process while pretending to have a treat on your nose. You will then want to incorporate this hand to your nose movement as your hand signal for watch me. Click and treat when your dog looks at you for at

least 1 second, then increase to 2 and 3 seconds, and click and treat after each goal. Repeat this about 10-15 times.

3. Increase the duration that your dog will continue to watch you while under the command. Click and treat as you progress. Try to keep your dog's attention for 5-10 seconds. Holding your dog's attention for this length of time usually results in the catalyst for him to move away from the area or to lose interest in the barking stimulus.

4. Now, practice the watch me command while you are walking around inside the house. Then practice this again outside near something he finds interesting. Also, practice this in a situation in which he would normally bark. Continue practicing in different situations and around other catalysts that you know will make your dog bark.

This is a great way to steer his attention to you and away from catalysts.

Other Solutions

1. When you notice something that normally makes your dog bark and he has not begun to bark, use the quiet command as a preemptive measure. For example, your dog regularly barks at the local skateboarder. When the trigger that provokes your dog's barking, the skateboarder, comes zooming by, use the command "Quiet", and click and treat. Click and treat your dog for every few seconds that he remains quiet.

Teach your dog that his barking trigger gets him a quiet command. Your dog will begin to associate the skateboarder with treats and gradually it will diminish his barking outbursts at the skateboarder. Then continue with the other barking catalysts.

2. If he frequently barks while a car is passing by, put a treat by his nose and then bring it to your nose. When he looks at you, click and treat him. Repeat this until he voluntarily looks at you when a car goes by and does not bark, and continue to treat him appropriately.

3. You can also reward your dog for calm behavior. When you see something or encounter something that he would normally bark at and he does not, click and treat your dog. Instead of treats, sometimes offer praise and affection. As a reminder, it is a good idea not to always use treats as rewards.

4. If you are out walking and your dog has not yet learned the quiet cue or is not responding to it, turn around and walk away from whatever is causing your dog to bark. When he calms down, offer a reward.

5. As a last resort use the citronella spray collar when your dog's barking cannot be controlled using the techniques that you have learned. Use this only when the barking is not associated with fear or aggression.

Your Dog Is Afraid, Aggressive, Lonely, Territorial or Hungover

Your dog may have outbursts when he feels territorial, aggressive, lonely or afraid. All of these negative behaviors can be helped with proper and early socialization, but occasionally they resurface.

Often rescue dogs have not been properly socialized and bring their negative behaviors into your home. Be patient while you are teaching your new dog proper etiquette. Some breeds, especially watch and guarding breeds, are prone to territorialism and it can be a challenge to limit their barking.

- As a temporary solution, you should first try to prevent outbursts by crating, gating, blocking windows, using fans or music to hide sounds and avoid taking your dog places that can cause these barking outbursts.

This is not a permanent solution, but is a helpful solution while you are teaching your dog proper barking etiquette. To allow your dog a chance to find his center, relax his mind and body, do this for about 7 to 10 days before beginning to train against barking.

Some Tips

1. If training is too stressful on you or your dog, or not going well, then you may want to hire a professional positive trainer for private sessions. When interviewing, tell him or her that you are using a clicker or reward-based training system and are looking for a trainer that uses the same type or similar methods.

2. Always remain calm, because a relaxed and composed alpha achieves great training outcomes. A confident, calm, cool and collected attitude that states you are unquestionably in charge goes a long way in training all commands.

It is important to help your dog to modify his thinking about what tends to upset him. Teach him that what he was upset about before now produces his favorite things.

Here is how

1. When the trigger appears in the distance, click and treat your dog. Keep clicking and treating your dog as the 2 of you proceed closer to the negative stimulus.

2. If he is territorially aggressive, teach him that the doorbell or a knock on the door means that that is his cue to get into his crate and wait for treats. You can do this by ringing the doorbell and luring your dog to his crate and, once he is inside the crate, giving him treats.

3. You can also lure your dog away from his fears. If you are out walking and encounter one of his triggers, put a treat to his nose and lead him out and away from the trigger zone.

4. Use the watch me command when you see him getting nervous or afraid. Click and treat him frequently for watching you.

5. Reward calm behavior with praise, toys, play or treats.

6. For the hangover, I recommend lots of sleep and water.

Your dog is frustrated, bored or both

All dogs including your dog Mini Aussie may become bored or frustrated. At these times, your dog may lose focus, not pay attention to you and spend time writing bad poetry in his journal.

A few things that can help prevent boredom and frustration are as follows.

1. Keep him busy and tire him out with chew toys, exercise, play and training. These things are a cure for most negative behaviors. A tired dog is usually happy to relax and enjoy quiet time.

2. Your pup should have at least 30 minutes of aerobic exercise per day. In addition to the aerobic exercise, each day he should have an hour of chewing and about 15 minutes of training. Keep it interesting for him with a variety of activities. It is, after all, the spice of life.

3. Use the command quiet or give your dog a time out.

4. As a last resort, you can break out the citronella spray collar.

Excited to play

- Like all of us, your puppy will get excited about play. Teach your dog that when he starts to bark, the playtime stops. Put a short leash on him and if he barks, use it to lead him out of play sessions. Put your dog in a time out or just stop playing with your dog. Reward him with more play when he calms down.

Armed with these many training tactics to curb and stop your dog barking, you should be able to gradually reduce your dog's barking and help him to understand that some things are not worth barking about. Gradually you will be able to limit the clicking and treating, but it is always good practice to reward your dog for not barking. Reward your dog with supersized treat servings for making the big breakthroughs.

28 Nipping

Friendly and feisty, little puppies nip for a few reasons such as when they are teething, playing or they want to get your attention. If you have acquired yourself a nipper, not to worry because in time most puppies will grow out of this behavior on their own. Other dogs, such as some bred for herding, nip as a herding instinct. They use this behavior to round up their animal charges, household animals and all human family members, especially children. Other dogs can acquire this annoying action by us allowing it to continue when they playfully nip at our heels.

You will want to avoid punishing or correcting your dog while he is working through the nipping stage, because this could eventually result in a strained relationship down the road. However, you will want to teach your puppy how delicate human skin is. Let your dog test it out and give him feedback. You can simply indicate your discomfort when he bites or nips by using an exclamation, such as, "Yipe!", "Youch!" or "Bowie!" in addition to a physical display of your pain by pulling back your hand, calf or ankle. This will usually be enough for your dog to understand that it is not an acceptable behavior.

After this action, it is important to cease offering any further attention to your dog, because this provides the possibility that the added attention will reinforce the negative behavior. If you act increasingly more sensitive to the nips, he will begin to understand that we humans are very sensitive and quickly respond with sudden vocal and physical displays of discomfort.

This is a very easy behavior to modify because we know the motivation behind it. The puppy wants to play and chew, and who is to blame him for this? Remember, it is important to give your dog access to a variety of chew toys and, when he nips, respond accordingly, then immediately walk away and ignore him. If he follows you and nips at your heels, give your dog a time out. Afterward, when your dog is relaxed, calm and in a gentle disposition, stay and play with him. Use the utmost patience with your puppy during this time, and keep in mind that this behavior will eventually pass.

Mini Aussies are not commonly known to be nippers such as Australian Cattle Dogs, and instead use body language and staring techniques to move stock, but you never know when a nipper might be in your midst.

Herding dogs that nip will not be easily dissuaded. For these breeds, it is not always possible to curb this behavior entirely, but you can certainly limit or soften it, eventually making them understand that nipping humans is a no-no, and very painful. To address this more thoroughly, between the ages of 4 and 5 months herding dogs can be enrolled in behavioral classes. This will reinforce your training and boost what you are training at home.

Preventing the Nippage

- Always have a chew toy in your hand when you are playing with your puppy. This way he learns that the right thing to bite and chew is the toy and not your hand or any other part of your body.

- Get rid of your puppy's excess energy by exercising him at least an hour each day. As a result, he will have less energy to nip.

- Make sure he is getting adequate rest and that he is not cranky from a lack of sleep. Twelve hours per day is good for dogs, and it seems for teenagers as well.

- Always have lots of interesting chew toys available to help your puppy to cope during the teething process.

- Teach your kids not to run away screaming from nipping puppies. They should walk away quietly or simply stay still. Children should never be left unsupervised around dogs.

- Play with your puppy in his gated puppy area. This makes it easier to walk away if he will not stop biting or mouthing you. This quickly reinforces his understanding that hard bites end play sessions.

- As a last resort, when the other interventions and methods discussed above are not working, you should increase the frequency of your use of a tieback to hold your dog in place within a gated or time-out area. If your dog is out of control with nipping or biting, and you have not yet trained him that biting is an unacceptable behavior, you may have to use this method until he is fully trained.

For example, you may want to use this when guests are over or if you simply need a break. Always use a tieback while your dog is under supervision and never leave him tied up alone. The tieback is a useful method and can be utilized as a tool of intervention when addressing other attention-getting behaviors like jumping, barking or the dreaded leg humping.

The best option during this time, early in his training, is to place him in a room with a baby gate blocking the doorway.

Instructing Around the "Nippage"

- Play with your dog and praise him for being gentle. When he nips say, "Yipe!" mimicking the sound of an injured puppy, and then immediately walk away. After the nipping, wait 1 minute and then return to give him another chance at play, or simply remain in your presence without nipping.

Practice this for 2 or 3 minutes, remembering to give everyone present or those who will have daily contact with your pup a chance to train him through play. It is crucial that puppies do not receive any reward for nipping. After an inappropriate bite or nip, all physical contact needs to be abruptly stopped, and quick and complete separation needs to take place so that your puppy receives a clear message.

- After your puppy begins to understand that bites hurt, and if he begins to give you a softer bite, continue to act hurt even if it doesn't. In time, your dog will understand that only the slightest pressures by mouth are permissible during play sessions. Continue practicing this until your puppy is only using the softest of bites, and placing limited tension upon your skin.

- Next, the goal is to decrease the frequency of mouthing. You can use the verbal cues of quit or off to signal that his mouth needs to release your appendage. Insist that the amount of time your puppy uses his mouth on you needs to decrease in duration, as well as the severity of pressure needs to decrease. If you need an incentive, use kibble or liver to reward him after you command and he obeys. Another reward for your puppy when releasing you from his mouth is to give him a chew or chew toy stuffed with food.

- The desired outcome of this training is for your puppy to understand that mouthing any human, if done at all, should be executed with the utmost care, and in such a manner that without question the pressure will not inflict pain or damage.

- Continue the training using the verbal cue of quit, until quit becomes a well-understood command, and your dog consistently complies when it is used. Take breaks every 20-30 seconds when playing and any type of mouthing occurs. The calm moments will allow excitement to wane and will help to reduce the chances of your dog excitably clamping down. Practice this frequently, and as a part of your regular training practice schedule. The result from successful training and knowing that your dog will release on command will give you peace of mind.

- If you have children, or are worried about the potential for injury due to biting, you can continue training in a way that your dog knows that mouthing is not permitted under any circumstance. This level of training prevents you from having to instruct a permissible mouthing pressure and therefore reduces your anxiety whenever your dog is engaged in play with family or friends. This of course nearly eliminates the potential for biting accidents.

Remain vigilant when visitors are playing with your dog. Monitor the play, and be especially attentive to the quality of the interaction, being alert that the session is not escalating into a rough and potentially forceful situation in which your dog might choose to use his mouth in an aggressive or harmful way.

You will need to decide the rules of engagement, and it will be your responsibility that others understand these rules. To avoid harm or injury it will be necessary for you to instruct visitors and family prior to play. Excessive biting also pertains to other dogs and animals; it should not be tolerated when used with pain inflicting force.

29 Digging Help

Some dogs are going to dig no matter what you do to stop it. For these diggers, this behavior is innate to them, so remember that these dogs have an urge to do what they do. Whether this behavioral trait is for hunting or foraging, it is deeply imbedded inside their DNA and it is something that cannot be easily turned off. Remember that when you have a digger for a dog, they tend to be excellent escape artists, so you will need to bury your perimeter fencing deep to keep them inside your yard or kennel.

Cold weather dogs, such as Huskies, Malamutes, Chows and other "spitz"-type dogs often dig a shallow hole in an area to lie down in, to either cool down or warm up. These dogs usually dig in a selected and distinct area, such as in the shade of a tree or shrub. Feral dogs mimic this to create sleeping spaces at night. I see this commonly with stray dogs living near beaches. In the mornings, you can see sleeping holes littering the beach where a number of dogs have slept.

Other natural diggers, such as Terriers and Dachshunds, are natural hunters and dig holes to bolt from or in which to hold prey at bay for their hunting companions. These breeds have been genetically bred for the specific purpose of digging into holes to chase rabbits, hares, badgers, weasels, and other burrowing animals.

Scent hounds, such as Beagles, Bassets and Bloodhounds, will dig under fences in pursuit of their quarry. This trait is not easily altered or trained away, but you can steer it into the direction of your choosing.

To combat dog escapes you will need to bury your fencing or chicken wire deep into the ground. It is suggested that 18-24 inches, or 46-61cm into the soil below the bottom edge of your fencing is sufficient, but we all know that a determined dog may even go deeper when in pursuit of quarry. Some dog owners will affix chicken wire at about 12 inches (30.5cm) up onto the fence, and then bury the rest down deep into the soil. Usually, when the digging dog reaches the wire, its efforts will be thwarted and it will stop digging.

Some dogs dig as an instinctive impulse to forage for food to supplement their diet, and this might be your dog's preference for digging up your garden. Because dogs are omnivorous, they will sometimes root out tubers, rhizomes, bulbs, or any other edible root vegetable that is buried in the soil. Even nuts buried by squirrels, newly sprouting grasses, the occasional rotting carcass or other attractive scents will be an irresistible aroma to their highly sensitive noses.

Other reasons dogs dig can be traced directly to boredom, lack of exercise, lack of mental and physical stimulation, and due to being improperly or under-socialized. Improperly socialized dogs can suffer from separation anxiety and other behavioral issues. Non-neutered dogs may dig an escape to chase a female in heat. Working breeds, for instance Border Collies, Australian Cattle Dogs, Shelties and others, can stir up all sorts of trouble if not kept busy. This trouble can include incessant digging.

It has been said that the smell of certain types of soil can also catch a dog's fancy. Fresh earth, moist earth, certain mulches, topsoil and even sand are all lures for the digger. If you have a digger, you should fence off the areas where you are using these alluring types of soil. These kinds of soil are often used in newly potted plants or when establishing a flowerbed or garden. The smell of dirt can sometimes attract a dog that does not have the strong digging gene, but when he finds out how joyful digging can be, beware - you can be responsible for the creation of your own "Frankendigger".

Proper socialization, along with plenty of mental and physical exercise, will help you in your fight against digging, but as we know, some diggers are going to dig no matter what the situation. Just in case your dog or puppy is an earnest excavator, here are some options to help you curb that urge.

Digging Solutions

Create a Digging Pit

A simple and fun solution is to dig a pit specifically for him or her to dig to their little heart's content. Select an appropriate location, and use a spade to turn over the soil a bit to loosen it up, mix in some sand to keep it loose as well to improve drainage, then surround it with stones or bricks to make it obvious by sight that this is the designated digging spot.

To begin training your dog to dig inside the pit, you have to make it attractive and worth their while. First bury bones, chews, or a favorite toy, then coax your dog on over to the pit to dig up some treasures. Keep a watchful eye each time you bring your dog out and do not leave him or her unsupervised during this training time.

It is important immediately to halt any digging outside of the pit. When they dig inside of the designated pit, be sure to reward them with treats and praise. If they dig elsewhere, direct them back to the pit. Be sure to keep it full of the soil-sand mixture and, if necessary, littered with their favorite doggie bootie. If your dog is not taking to the pit idea, an option is to make the other areas where they are digging temporarily less desirable, such as covering them with chicken wire, which will make the pit look highly tantalizing, like a doggie digging paradise.

Buried Surprises

Two other options are leaving undesirable surprises in the unwanted holes your dog has begun to dig. A great deterrent is to place your dog's own doodie into the holes that he has dug, and when your dog returns to complete his job, he will not enjoy the gift you have left him, thus deterring him from further digging.

Another excellent deterrent is to place an air-filled balloon inside the hole and then cover it with soil. When your dog returns to his undertaking and his little paws burst the balloon, the resulting loud "POP!" sound will startle him, resulting in your dog reconsidering the importance of the digging mission. After a few of these shocking noises, you should have a dog that thinks twice before digging up your bed of pansies.

Shake Can Method

This method requires a soda can or another container filled with rocks, bolts or coins. Remember to place tape or apply the cap over the open end to keep the objects inside.

Keep this "rattle" device nearby so that when you let your dog out into the yard you can take it with you to your clandestine hiding spot. While hidden out of sight, simply wait until our dog begins to dig. Immediately at the time of digging, take that can of coins and shake it vigorously, thereby startling your dog. Repeat the action each time your dog begins to dig, and after a few times your dog should refrain from further soil removal. Remember, the goal is to startle and to distract your dog at the time they initiate their digging and not to terrorize your little friend.

Shake can instructions

1. Shake it quickly once or twice and then stop. The idea is to make a sudden and disconcerting noise that is unexpected by your dog who is in the process of digging. If you continue shaking the can, it will become an ineffective technique.

2. Beware not to overuse this method. Remember your dog can become desensitized to the sound, and thus ignore the prompt.

3. Sometimes, it is important to supplement this method by using commands, such as "No" or "Stop".

4. Focus these techniques, targeting only the behavior (e.g. digging) that you are trying to eliminate.

5. Sometimes, a noise made by a can with coins inside may not work, but perhaps using a different container filled with nuts and bolts or other metal items will. Dogs might find the tone/pitch of certain metals more disconcerting.

Examples are soda or coffee cans that are filled with coins, nuts, bolts or other metal objects. You might have to experiment to get an effective and disruptive sound. If the noise you make sets off prolonged barking instead of a quick startled bark, then the sound is obviously not appropriate. If your dog does begin to bark after you make the noise, use the quiet command immediately after and never forget to reward your dog when he stops the barking, thereby reinforcing the wanted behavior.

I hope that these methods will assist you in controlling or guiding your 4-legged landscaper in your desired direction. Anyone that has had a digger for a dog knows it can be challenging. Just remember that tiring them out with exercise and games is often the easiest and most effective way of curbing unwanted behaviors.

~ Paps

PART III

30 Basic Care for Mini Australian Shepherds

Oral maintenance, nail clipping, and other grooming will depend upon you and your dog's activities. We all know our dogs love to roll and run through all sorts of ugly messes and put obscene things into their mouths and then afterward run up to lick us.

Below is a list of the basic grooming care your dog requires. Most basic care can easily be done at home by you, but if you are unsure or uncomfortable about something, seek tutelage and in no time you will be clipping, trimming and brushing your dog like a professional.

It is vital that handling training begin at the onset of bringing your puppy home because this will aid in all grooming, training, socialization and potential medical procedures. Early handling of your dog is crucial for grooming because it will allow you or the groomer to perform grooming while manipulating all of your dog's body parts with little to no resistance. Most owners should be able to learn and perform some or all of the grooming techniques themselves.

If you are grooming your dog up on a table or slippery surface, first place a non-slip cloth or mat over that area so that your dog doesn't slip or move during the grooming process. This will avoid potential injury.

Coat Brushing

Daily brushing of your dog's coat can be done or at least a minimum of three to four times a week depending upon the condition of the coat. During heavy shedding twice yearly, daily brushing is recommended. Daily brushing is not required, but it is healthy for the coat and skin. Additionally, it aids in regularly inspecting your dog for ticks, fleas, lumps, or rashes.

Mini Aussies have a double coat that is not high maintenance and sheds dirt well. They are moderate to heavy shedders so regular brushing will keep your hair mess to a minimum and keep their skin and coat healthy. Shearing is not recommended or necessary, their double coat protects them during all climate conditions, so it is best to leave it long.

Brushing with a slicker brush 3-4 times per week is a good habit to get into, but at least brush twice weekly to keep tangles to a minimum and their coat healthy. Their coats do pick up burs and critters, which is why I recommend 3-4 times per week to brush and inspect. The goal is to keep tangles from turning into mats that are time consuming to remove and often require scissoring out of the coat.

Use a long tooth undercoat rake after brushing with the slicker brush. When you find tangles, gently work them with your fingers and slicker brush to untangle. The undercoat rake is to brush deep into the coat down to the skin but not scraping the skin but using a motion that is up and out from the skin. If your dog has tangle issues, a metal-toothed comb with wide and close spaced teeth helps work tangles out.

Mini Aussies do not require much trimming on their bodies but some trimming around the top and bottom of their paws can be done if the hair grows to long. Always use caution on the pad area, in this area many people use clippers instead of scissors. Additionally, if you choose you can trim some of the tail, ears and leg areas to create a uniform look.

When brushing, first place your dog into a position that is comfortable for both. You can either have your dog lie down on his side, or stand if he does not mind. I prefer standing as it allows easier access and better angles. Begin brushing at the head and brush in the direction that the coat flows all the way to the tail tip. If your dog is lying down, then roll them to the others side and repeat.

Always be patient and move slowly when grooming your dog's head and muzzle area, the eyes, ears, nose and mouth are all sensitive areas that can incur harm. Before you decide to groom your Mini Aussie yourself, learn the proper way to use shears and scissors when trimming around the head, muzzle and body. Depending upon the style you choose some of the grooming equipment can vary.

Bathing

Regular but not frequent bathing is essential. Much depends upon your dog's coat. Natural coat oils are needed to keep your dog's coat and skin moisturized. Never bathe your dog too frequently and brushing before bathing is recommended. Depending upon what your dog has been into, a bath once every month or two is adequate.

- Supplies – Dog-specific shampoo, 3-4 towels and a nonslip bathmat for inside the tub.

- Shampoo – Use a dog shampoo made specifically for sensitive skin. This helps avoid any type of potential skin allergy, eye discomfort or worsening pre-existing skin conditions.

- Coax your dog into the tub and shut the door, just in case he is not in the mood, or decides to bolt outside while still wet. We have all experienced this.

- Use warm water, never hot water. Hot water tends to irritate the skin and can cause your dog to itch and then scratch. Do not use cold water on your dog.

- Apply enough shampoo to create lather over the body, but take care not to use too much so that rinsing is difficult and time consuming. Rub into a lather while avoiding the eyes and ears.

- Bathe the head area last.

- Rinse repeatedly and thoroughly to avoid skin irritation.

- Thoroughly dry your dog by using a towel. If it is cold outside you will want to finish by using a hair dryer on a low setting. Additionally, a slicker brush can be used while drying, remembering to brush in the direction of the hair growth.

Nail trimming

For optimal foot health, your dog's nails should be kept short. There are special clippers that are needed for nail trimming that are designed to avoid injury. You can start trimming when your dog is a puppy, and you should have no problems. However, if your dog still runs for the hills or squirms like an eel at trimming time, then your local groomer or veterinarian can do this procedure.

Dog's nails are composed of a hard outer shell named the horn and a soft cuticle in the center known as the quick. The horn has no nerves and thus has no feeling. The quick is composed of blood vessels and nerves, and therefore needs to be avoided.

Black nails make the quick harder to identify. White nails allow the quick to be recognized by its pink coloring. Dogs that spend a lot of time walking and running on rough surfaces tend to have naturally shortened quicks. Furthermore, the quick grows with the nail, so diligent nail trimming will keep the quick receded.

- Identify where the quick is located in your dog's nails. The object will be to trim as close (2mm) to the quick as possible without nipping the quick and causing your dog pain and possibly bleeding.

- To identify the quick in black nails, begin cutting small pieces from the end of the nail and examine underneath the nail. When you see a uniform gray oval appear at the top of the cut surface, then stop further cutting. Behind the gray is where the quick is located, if you see pink then you have passed the gray and arrived at the quick. If you have done this, your dog is probably experiencing some discomfort. The goal is to stop cutting when you see the gray.

-File the cut end to smooth the surface.

- If you accidentally cut into the quick, apply styptic powder. If this is not available, cornstarch or flour can be used as a substitute.

- If your dog challenges your cutting, be diligent and proceed without verbal or physical abuse, and reward him after successful trimming is completed. If you encounter the occasional challenge, your diligence should curtail the objection. If you manage never to cut into your dog's quick, this helps prevent any negative associations with the process, but some dogs simply do not enjoy the handling of their paws or nail trimming.

Ear cleaning

You should clean your dog's ears at least once a month, but be sure to inspect them every few days for bugs such as mites and ticks and look for any odd discharge that can be an indication of infection, which would require a visit to the vet. Remember to clean the outer ear only using a damp cloth or a cotton swab doused with mineral oil.

Eye cleaning

Whenever you are grooming your dog, check their eyes for any signs of damage or irritation. Other signals for eye irritation are if your dog is squinting, scratching or pawing at their eyes. You should contact your veterinarian if you notice that the eyes are cloudy, red or have a yellow or green discharge.

Use a moist cotton ball to clean any discharge from the eye. Avoid putting anything irritating around or into your dog's eyes.

Brushing teeth

Pick up a specially designed canine tooth brush and cleaning paste. Clean your dog's teeth as frequently as daily. Try to brush your dog's teeth a minimum of a few times per week.

If your dog wants no part of having his or her teeth brushed, try rubbing his teeth and gums with your finger. After he is comfortable with this, you can then put some paste on your finger, allow him to smell and lick it, then repeat rubbing his teeth and gums with your finger. After he is comfortable with your finger, repeat with the brush. In addition, it is important to keep plenty of chews around to promote the oral health of your pooch. When your dog is 2-3 years old, he or she may need their first professional teeth cleaning.

Anal sacs

These sacs are located on each side of a dog's anus. If you notice your dog scooting his rear or frequently licking and biting at his anus, the anal sacs may be impacted. When you notice this, it is time to release some fluid from them using a controlled method. If you are not comfortable doing this, you can ask your veterinarian how to diagnose and treat this issue.

Both the male and female dogs have anal glands and they are found directly beneath the skin that surrounds the anal muscles. The other name for them is scent glands. These glands tell other dogs the mood of a dog, their health and gender, which is why so much butt sniffing goes on between dogs.

To release the fluid when they are enlarged, it is good practice to place your Mini Aussie inside a bathtub. The fluid is pungent and brownish in color so a tub protects anything that might come into contact with it.

Place a finger on each side of the sac, then apply pressure upwards and inwards towards the rectum, and this is when you should see the fluid come out. If, for some reason, fluid does not come out, seek assistance because if they are enlarged they need to be emptied.

31 A Dog's Nutrition

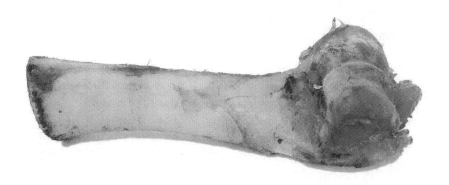

As for nutrition, humans study it, practice it, complain about it, but usually give into the science and common sense of it. Like humans, dogs have their own nutritional needs and are subject to different theories and scientific studies.

In the beginning, there were wild packs of canines everywhere and they ate anything that they could get their claws and teeth into. Similar to human survival, dogs depended upon meat from kills, grasses, berries and other edibles that nature provided. Thankfully, nature is still providing all the food animals need.

In the mid to late 1800s a middle class blossomed out of the industrial revolution. This new class with its burgeoning wealth had extra money to spend and started taking on dogs as house pets. Unwittingly they created an enterprise out of feeding the suddenly abundant household pets.

Noting that sailors' biscuits kept well for long periods, James Spratt began selling his own recipe of hard biscuits for dogs in London, and shortly thereafter took his new product to New York City. It is believed that he single-handedly started the American dog food business. This places the dog food and kibble industry at just over 150 years old, and is now an annual multi-billion dollar business.

All the while, we know that any farm, feral or other dog that can kill something and eat it will do just that. Nothing has changed throughout the centuries. Raw meat does not kill dogs, so it is safe to say that raw food diets will not either. If you are a bit tentative about the idea of raw foods, cooking the meats you serve your dog is a viable option.

Feeding Your Puppy and Adult Dog

To check if your puppy has its proper dietary needs met, make sure that your puppy is active, alert and is showing good bone and muscle development. To understand the correct portion to feed your dog, ask the breeder to show you the portion that they feed their puppies. Then observe whether your puppy is quickly devouring their food and then acting as though he wants and needs more. If so, then increase the portion a little until you find the correct serving. If your puppy is eating quickly, then begins to nibble, and finally leaves food in the bowl, then you are overfeeding him.

As you adjust the food portion to less or more, observe whether your puppy is gaining or losing weight so that you can find the proper portion of food to serve during feeding times. Very active puppies tend to burn lots of energy and this is one reason that a puppy might need a little extra food in their bowl. The suggested portions are on the food containers, but this world is not a one-size-fits-all place. Observation and logging those observations is needed to determine the correct portions for your dog.

Most agree that puppies should not leave their mothers until they are at least 8 weeks old. This allows their mother's milk to boost their immune system by supplying the antibodies and nutrition that are needed to become a healthy dog. Around 3 to 4 weeks old puppies should begin eating some solid food in conjunction with their mother's milk because this helps their digestion process begin to adjust to solid foods, making the transition from mother's milk to their new home and foods easier.

Puppies are going to eat 4 times a day up until about 8 weeks. At 8 weeks, they can still be fed 4 times a day or you can reduce it to 3 times. Split the recommended daily feeding portion into thirds. Puppies' nutritional requirements differ from adult dogs so select a puppy food that has the appropriate balance of nutrients that puppies require. Puppy food should continue to support healthy growth, digestion and the immune system. Supplying your growing puppy with the correct amount of calories, protein and calcium is part of a well-balanced diet.

When choosing your puppy's feeding times, choose the times that you know will be the best for you to feed your puppy. Feeding on a regular schedule is one part of the overall consistency that you are establishing for your puppy so that he will know that as the leader you will reliably satisfying his needs. After setting the feeding schedule, remain as close to those times as possible. For example, 7 am, noon, and again at 5pm are good times if that fits your schedule. An earlier dinnertime helps your puppy to digest then eliminate before their bedtime.

During the 3 to 6-month puppy stage, teething can alter your puppy's eating habits. Some pups may not feel like eating due to pain, so it is your responsibility to remain diligent in your job to provide them with all of their nutritional requirements and confirm that they are eating.

Hint: Soaking their dry food in water for 10-15 minutes before feeding will soften it and make it easier for your puppy to eat. This avoids suddenly introducing different, softer foods to your puppy and avoids the unknown consequences of that such as diarrhea and gas.

At 6 months to a year old, your puppy still requires high quality, nutritionally charged foods. Consult your breeder or veterinarian about the right time to switch to an adult food.

When you switch to an adult food, continue to choose the highest quality food that contains a specified meat, and not only byproducts. Avoid unnecessary artificial additives. In many cases, higher quality dog foods will allow you to serve smaller portions because more of the food is being used by your dog and not just flowing through him. Fillers are often not digested and this requires feeding your dog larger portions.

Additionally, follow the alpha guideline that states that humans always eat first. This means that the humans of the family finish their meal entirely and clear the table before feeding their dogs, or feed your dog a couple of hours before you and your family eat. This establishes and continues the precedence that all humans are above the dog in the pecking order.

Help Identifying Dog Food Quality

- The first ingredient or, at a minimum, the second, should specify meat or meat meal, NOT byproduct.

- "What is a byproduct?" Unless specified on the label, a byproduct can be leftover parts of animals and contain parts of hooves, feet, skin, eyes or other animal body parts.

- Beware of ingredients that use wording such as animal and meat instead of specific words like beef or chicken.

- "Meal" when listed in ingredients is something that has been weighed after the water was taken out, an example would be chicken meal. This means it has been cooked with a great amount of water reduction occurring in the process, and thus it is providing more actual meat and protein per weight volume.

  As an example, if the dog food package only states "beef" in the ingredients, it refers to the pre-cooking weight. This means that after cooking, less meat will be present in the food.

- A label that states "beef" first then "corn meal" second, is stating that the food probably contains a lot more corn than beef.

  Corn is not easily digested nor does it offer much in the way of nutrients that are vital to a dog's health. Furthermore, it has been linked to other health issues, and dogs are not designed to eat corn and grains in high doses. Try your best to avoid corn, wheat and soy in your dog's food. The higher quality more expensive foods are often worth the cost to advance your dog's health.

- If you decide to change dog food formulas or brands, a gradual change over is recommended, especially if your dog has a sensitive stomach. This is done by mixing some of the old with the new, and then throughout the week gradually increasing the amount of the new food.

An example schedule of changing dog foods

Day 1-2 Mix ¼ new with ¾ old foods

Day 2-4 Mix ½ new with ½ old

Day 5-6 Mix ¾ new with ¼ old

Day 7 100% of the new dog food

The Switch - Moving From Puppy to Adult Food

When your puppy is ready to make the switch from puppy to adult dog food, you can follow the same procedure above or shorten it to a 4 to 5 day switchover. During the switch, be observant of your dog's stools and health.

If your dog appears not to handle the new food formula well, then your options are to change the current meat to a different meat, or try a different formula or brand. Avoid returning to the original puppy food. If you have any concerns or questions, consult your veterinarian or breeder.

Raw Foods

Let us first remember that our dogs, pals, best friends and comedic actors are meant to eat real foods such as meat. Their DNA does not dictate them to eat dry cereals that were concocted by humans in white lab coats. These cereal-based and meat byproduct ingredients may keep our pets alive, but in many cases they won't thrive at an optimum level.

There are many arguments for the benefits of real and raw foods. Sure it is more work, but isn't their health worth it? It is normal, not abnormal, to be feeding your dog a living food diet; it is believed that it will greatly boost their immune system and overall health. A raw food diet is based off pre-dog food diets and is a return to their wild hunting and foraging days and pre-manmade biscuit foods.

I travel a lot throughout South East Asia and the majority of dogs there eat what their humans eat and are doing just fine.

There are different types of raw food diet. There are raw meats that you can prepare at home by freeze-drying or freezing them and then easily thawing them and feeding them to your dog, commercially pre-packaged frozen raw foods, or offering up an entire animal.

All of these diets take research and careful attention so that you are offering your dog all that he needs, and something that his body can easily tolerate. Correct preparation of raw food diets needs to be understood, for example, it is suggested that vegetables are cut into very small pieces or even pureed.

Raw food diets amount to foods that are not cooked or sent through a processing plant. With some research, you can make a decision on what you think is the best type of diet for your dog. For your dog's health and for their optimal benefit, it is worth the effort to read up on a raw food diet, a mix of kibble and raw food, or a raw and cooked food diet mix. All foods, dry, wet or raw contain a risk, as they can all contain contaminants and parasites.

The known benefits are fewer preservatives, chemicals, hormones, steroids and the addition of fruits and vegetables into their diet. Physically your dog can have firmer stools, reduced allergies, improved digestion, a healthier coat and skin, and overall improved health.

Some of the negative attributes are the lack of convenience versus kibble and potential bacterial contamination. However, dogs are at a lowered risk for salmonella and E. coli than humans are. A dog's digestive system is more acidic and less prone to such diseases; the greater risk is to the preparer. Many experts state that the overall risk of a properly prepared raw food diet is minimal.

There is a process named high pressure pasteurization (HPP) which most pre-prepared raw food brands utilize in their processing that does not use heat but eliminates harmful bacteria without killing off the good bacteria.

Rules of thumb to follow for a raw food diet

1. Before switching, make sure that your dog has a healthy gastrointestinal tract.

2. Be smart, and do not leave meat unrefrigerated for prolonged periods.

3. To be safe, simply follow human protocol for food safety. Toss out the smelly, slimy or the meat and other food items that just do not seem fit for consumption.

4. Keep it balanced. Correct amount of vitamins and minerals, fiber, antioxidants and fatty acids. Note any medical issues your dog has and possible diet correlations.

5. If switching from bag or can, a gradual switchover between foods is recommended to allow their GI track to adjust. Use new foods as a treat, and then watch his stools to see how your dog is adjusting.

6. Take note of the size and type of bones you throw to your dog. Not all dogs do well with real raw bones because slivers, splinters and small parts can become lodged in their digestive tracts. Always provide the freshest bones possible to dogs. Never give dogs cooked bones.

7. Freezing meats for 3 days, similar to sushi protocol, can help kill unwanted pathogens or parasites.

8. Remember to be vigilant, and take note of your observations about what is working and not working with your dog's food changes. If your dog has a health issue, your veterinarian will thank you for your detailed note taking.

9. Like us humans, most dogs do well with a variety of foods. There is no one-size-fits-all diet.

10. Before switching over, please read about raw food diets and their preparation and follow all veterinary guidelines.

"BARF®" is an acronym that means biologically appropriate raw food. It is a complete and carefully balanced blend of raw meat, fruits, vegetables and bone. The formula mimics what nature designed for our pets to thrive in the wild. The result is a pet free of allergies, digestive problems and full of life!

In summary, the first line of defense against disease is feeding your dog a proper diet which includes feeding them premium dry food, canned food, raw food (or BARF diet), home-cooked food or any combination of these.

Vitamins – Nutrients - Minerals

According to nutritional scientists and veterinarian health professionals, your dog needs 20 amino acids, 10 of which are essential. At least 36 nutrients and a couple of extra may be needed to combat certain afflictions. Your dog's health depends upon the intake of the following nutrients. Read labels and literature to take stock of the foods you provide your canine.

It may take time to understand what kind of diet your dog will thrive on. Do your best to include in your dog's daily diet all 36 nutrients mentioned here, all of which can come from fruits, veggies, kibble, raw foods, and yes, even good table scraps. You will soon discover that your dog has preferred foods.

For your dog to maintain optimum health and have a healthy GI tract, he needs a well-rounded diet with a good balance of exercise, rest, socializing, care and love.

36 Nutrients for dogs:

1. 10 essential amino acids – Arginine, Histidine, Isoleucine, Leucine, Lysine, Methionine, Phenylalanine, Threonine, Tryptophan, and Valine.

2. 11 vitamins – A, D, E, B1, B2, B3, B5, B6, B12, Folic Acid, and Choline.

3. 12 minerals – Calcium, Phosphorus, Potassium, Sodium, Chloride, Iron, Magnesium, Copper, Manganese, Zinc, Iodine, and Selenium.

4. Fat – Linoleic Acid

5. Omega 6 Fatty Acid

6. Protein

Please take the time to REVIEW this Mini Australian Shepherd training guide and tell others about the positive information inside.

Review now by going to the Amazon page below and posting your

POSITIVE REVIEW

My family thanks you,

Paul

32 Final Thoughts

Believe me, this is not everything that there is to know about dogs. Training your Mini Australian Shepherd is a lifelong endeavor. There are myriad other methods, tricks, tools and things to teach and learn with your dog. You are never finished, but this is half of the fun of having a dog, as he or she is a constant work in progress. Your dog is living art.

If your training experience is anything similar to mine, there will be days and times when you think your dog will never catch on or be interested in participating and learning. I hope that you are able to work through the difficult times and the result will be that you and your dog understand one another at a high level, resulting in you having command of your dog.

Owning and befriending our dogs is a lifetime adventurous commitment that is worthwhile and rewarding on every level. It seems as though many times Axel knows what I am thinking and acts or reacts accordingly, but he and I are together more than I am with most of my other family members. Through the good and the bad times, he always makes me smile, and sometimes when he is being the most difficult I smile the biggest. He is such a foolhardy, loveable, intelligent, and clownish dog, how could anyone be sad around him?

Remember, it is important to learn to think like your dog. Having patience with your dog, as well as with yourself, is vital. If you do this right, you will have a relationship and a bond that will last for years. The companionship of a dog can bring joy and friendship like none other. Keep this book handy and reference it often. In addition, look for other resources, such as training books, and utilize like-minded experienced friends with dogs that can share their successes and failures. Never stop broadening your training skills. Your efforts will serve to keep you and your Mini Australian Shepherd happy and healthy for a long, long time.

Thanks for reading! I hope that you enjoyed this as much as I have enjoyed writing it. If this training guide informed you how to train your dog, please review this guide and tell others about the positive information in it. I am always striving to improve both my writing and training skills. I look forward to reading your comments.

No dogs were injured during the writing of this book. ☺

About the Author

Paul Allen Pearce is the author of many training books about specific dog breeds. Paul comes from a family of dog lovers that often took in strays. Both of his parents grew up with many animals and passed on intergenerational knowledge to their children.

At an early age, Paul and his siblings were taught to care and train their family pets. Raised around all sorts of animals, his curiosity to work with dogs grew. After returning to the U.S. and purchasing his own dog, he realized he didn't know as much as he could, thus began his journey into full-time dog training and research.

Dog training is his passion. He loves dogs, animals, and the wonders of nature. He says it's a pleasure to write about his passion and share what he has learned. He hopes that his readers enjoy and learn from what he has learned, thus enabling them to improve their relationships with their dogs.

Traveling through 30 countries and many U.S. states has helped him to broaden his perspective regarding animal behavior and treatment. He asks that people care for all animals, not just their loving dogs.

He spends his free time outdoors with his dogs, exploring nature and expanding his knowledge of life and dog training.

Other Books

"Don't Think BE - Alpha Dog Secrets Revealed"

**"Puppy Training Stuff - The 14 Puppy Essentials
Your Puppy Needs Now"**

**"No Brainer Dog Trainer"
(Breed-specific dog training series)**

Content Attributions

Photos: We wish to thank all of the photographers for sharing their photographs via Creative Commons Licensing.

COVER
Adobe Stock

BIO
Adobe Stock

PROBLEM BEHAVIORRS
pxhere.com / CC any use

EFFECTIVE MINI AUSTRALIAN TRAINING
Stimulating activities
pxhere.com / CC any use

DOWN
https://commons.wikimedia.org/wiki/File%3AMiniature_Australian_Shepherd_blue_merle.jpg
https://upload.wikimedia.org/wikipedia/commons/5/5f/Miniature_Australian_Shepherd_blue_merle.jpg
By Mike from Baltimore, USA (How About Now?) [CC BY 2.0
(http://creativecommons.org/licenses/by/2.0)], via Wikimedia Commons

SIT
Adobe Stock

STAY
Pixabay.com CC any use

BASIC CARE
https://upload.wikimedia.org/wikipedia/commons/a/a7/Miniature_Australian_Shepherd_red_tricolour.JPG
By Jillian Schoenfeld (Jillian Schoenfeld) [Public domain], via Wikimedia Commons

FINAL THOUGHTS
https://commons.wikimedia.org/wiki/File%3ABlue_Merle_Miniature_American_Shepherd_with_Frisbee.jpg_https://upload.wikimedia.org/wikipedia/commons/2/2f/Blue_Merle_Miniature_American_Shepherd_with_Frisbee.jpg_By Mullinspw (Own work) [CC0], via Wikimedia Commons

Legal Disclaimer

The author of "Think Like a Dog" books, Paul Allen Pearce, is in no way responsible at any time for the actions of your pet, not now or in the future. Animals, without warning, may cause injury to humans and/or other animals. Paul Allen Pearce is not responsible for attacks, bites, maulings, nor any other viciousness or any and all other damages.

We strongly recommend that you exercise caution for the safety of yourself, the animal, and all those around the animal while working with your dog. We are not liable for any animal or human medical conditions or results obtained from training.

While all attempts have been made to verify the information provided in this publication, neither the author nor the publisher assume any responsibility for errors, omissions or contrary interpretations of the subject matter contained herein. The publisher and author assume no responsibility or liability whatsoever on the behalf of any purchaser or reader of the material provided. The owner of this dog training guide assumes any, and all risks associated with the methodology described inside the dog-training guidebook.

Made in the USA
Columbia, SC
08 December 2024

48732360R00109